THE BREAKTHROUGH FACTOR

*Overcome Your Emotional Barriers
and Break Through to Success*

JEFFERY COMBS

[handwritten: 3/31/2019 → finished it 4/9/19 after reading "Letting Go" by David Hawkins]

[handwritten: KATHY I AM HONORED TO BE YOUR COACH + FRIEND Jeff C]

GOLDEN MASTERMIND
SEMINARS
INC.

Published by Golden Mastermind Seminars Inc.
www.goldenmastermind.com

Printed in the United States of America

5 4 3 2 1

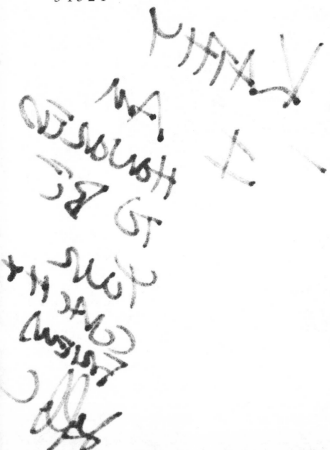

Dedicated to the individuals committed to living their best life and becoming the person they deserve to be

TABLE OF CONTENTS

FOREWORD

Back in 1996 I was just getting started in free enterprise, and the week of Christmas, I ran an ad in *USA Today*. The trajectory of my life changed forever by running that one little ad.

In life and in business, one moment can alter your destiny.

I was very fortunate that a young man by the name of Jeffery Combs responded to a *USA Today* ad that ran on December 27, 1996.

Jeffery went through the information process we had in place. Because I was just getting started in free enterprise myself, I didn't have a track record of success to present to Jeffery, but we had a system in place, and Jeffery went through that system. He recognized an opportunity with our business and wanted to get started, but here's the issue: Jeffery didn't have the money to get started.

It was around two thousand dollars to get started with us back then, and Jeffrey was just coming off a devastating business experience. With his previous company he had produced at a record level, only to discover they weren't going to pay him. They had taken incredible advantage of him, and it was on the heels of that experience that he responded to my *USA Today* ad. It changed my life forever.

It transformed my life in such a way that even Jeffery doesn't realize the full impact he had on my life.

I bring this up because I witnessed firsthand Jeffery's rise from overwhelming odds to become the number-one income producer in my entire organization worldwide.

Talk about a Breakthrough to Success!

Jeffery immediately started doing things that had never been done before in that organization. He started producing results that nobody had ever produced. I share this with you because I think it's important for you recognize that the Jeffery is the *genuine article*.

What he says that he's done he's done, and it's amazing to me that, as accomplished as Jeffery is, he doesn't lead with ego; he's always *led with the heart* to make an impact in the lives of people.

I say this because we live in a time where there's so much fakery in the media today. People pose in front of airplanes that don't belong to them; they pose in front of cars they do not own; and they Photoshop fake bank accounts; and standing in the midst of this is one of the most *authentic voices of our generation*.

Not only has Jeffery done everything he says he's done, he has done so with a spirit of excellence.

I was there, and I witnessed Jeffery's rise against overwhelming odds at one of the worst times in his life. I witnessed Jeffery experience breakthrough after breakthrough until he reached the top in that organization.

Jeffery became number one not because he had his own breakthroughs, but he was highly skilled at assisting others on his team to experience their own breakthroughs to success.

Jeffrey was highly skilled at helping his team members "break through" to six-figure and multiple six-figure incomes. I'm talking about folks that would have *never* have hit six- figure incomes without Jeffery's intervention in their life.

Fed Ex drivers, mechanics, personal trainers, stay-at-home moms—as long as they had heart and desire, Jeffery was able to empower them to produce at record levels.

Jeffery developed the proven blueprint to their breakthough.

I believe in "earning the right" to teach whatever it is that you are teaching or advocating others to do.

To be clear with you, Jeffery Combs, has *earned the right* to teach on this topic.

Has he ever!

By reading this book, your life will be *transformed* by somebody who has had the real, authentic, "in the trenches" experience of starting from nothing and producing incredible results *in a very short period of time*, first for himself and then for others.

A good friend of mine once told me that "the truth has a distinctive sound to it and people recognize that sound when they hear it."

As you read this book, you will hear that *distinctive sound of truth*.

This is your moment in time—you're exactly where I was back on December 27, 1996, when Jeffery Combs entered my life.

Whether you know it or not, your Breakthrough to Success is here!

—TC Bradley

CEO and founder, InstantCelebrityStatus.com

INTRODUCTION

This book is designed to guide you through the breakthrough process. It is the culmination of my experiences and my knowledge of how to overcome life's obstacles. It contains more than thirty years of my discoveries of personal growth and development, alcohol and drug addiction recovery, my failures and successes in entrepreneurship, and over twenty years of success and addiction coaching.

In December 1988, I hit rock bottom. I ended up in a county detox with delirium tremors from my alcohol abuse. I made a promise to myself that if I survived, I would get back to living my dreams and commit to my recovery.

At thirty-one years old, I got clean and sober, but I hadn't yet addressed the cause of my addictions. I abstained from alcohol but struggled with the emotional and psychological issues that created my addictions. Manifestations of anxiety, resentment, disappointment, and anger were still present in my life. They were causing challenges in my ability to succeed as an entrepreneur.

In 1990 I started my first network marketing business. I spent the next eight years mastering the skills of free enterprise. I went through several failed business ventures and ended up with $100,000 of credit card debt. I was at a point where I had to detach myself from those negative thought patterns if I was going to succeed in free enterprise.

I knew I was in the right industry, but I wasn't the right person yet. The years 1995 and 1996 were the most challenging years of my financial life, but they were also the most rewarding spiritually and personal growth-wise. By the end of 1996, at what appeared to be my darkest hour, a ray of light broke through. I had crossed over from resistance into flow, and I began to flourish instead of struggle. Within a twelve-month period, I created a seven-figure income and paid off all my debt.

In 1998 I transitioned from full-time network marketer to full-time inspirational speaker, writer, and success coach. Today I get great satisfaction by being able to inspire my clients. Most importantly, I'm skilled at assisting people to understand their addictions.

As a coach, I assist my clients to understand the cause that creates the effect. I show people how to separate events from their past and the feelings that were shaped by them. I not only coach network marketers, I mentor people from all walks of life. Addictions are my niche in assisting people to understand why they get emotionally stuck. Watching people break through inspires me. And I have a high rate of success in assisting people to release the conscious and unconscious anxieties that keep them perpetuating the same set of feelings over and over.

I wrote this book to assist you with your breakthrough process and assist you to uncover why you do what you do. I want you to understand how past events from your life have created your conditioned behavior. The more you understand how your brain works, the better chance you will have to work with it to create change rather than struggle against it.

In these pages I will share more of my personal path and stories of my clients. I will give you specific examples of cause and effect. You may find many of the scenarios to be relatable to your life or someone close to you. Some of the most profound breakthroughs often come from seeing yourself in others as a mirror.

As I began to study the neuroscience of physical and emotional addictions, my breakthough process accelerated. I have shared the stage and spent quality time with both John Assaraf and Dr. Joe Dispenza—two of the top neuroscience experts in the field today. I incorporate their content into my teaching and speaking and highly endorse both of them.

Breaking through is not a one-time event, although a breakthrough can come in an instant. My intention for you in reading this book is that you gain the emotional resiliency skills to stay present and forge ahead even when you are challenged with adversity. The goal is to break through instead of breaking down.

In this book, you will gain a greater understanding of your emotions. You will learn skills and techniques to assist you with the breakthrough process. The break-through process is more of an emotional process than a physical one. You won't require a hammer to break down a wall.

The skills you will learn in this book are life skills. They are emotional skills and recovery skills. When you are committed to being the best human being you can be, the breakthough process never ends.

There are common themes that hold people back from breaking through. Most people tiptoe through life never really living it to the fullest. They hope and wish that their dreams will come true. Instead of pursuing life, they let life happen to them. My goal for you in reading this book is that you learn to create your life. I want you to live it one day at a time being the best you can be. Once you understand the process, you can make breakthroughs a way of life.

As part of this book, you will gain access to free additional audio and video training materials. These trainings are meant to enhance your breakthrough process. You can find them at https://goldenmastermind. com/breakthrough-factor.

ONE
WHAT IS A BREAKTHROUGH?

What is a breakthrough? A breakthrough is an event that happens in an instant. It's a change in consciousness. It's a heightened understanding. It's a light switch flipping on in your mind, enlightening you to a concept you couldn't see or understand before. You will find throughout this book, breaking through is typically not physical. It's not linear. It's letting go of an old way of thinking, feeling, or being.

Some people seek out ways to break through, while others must break though because they are facing dire consequences—which was the case for me. I spent twenty years of my life as a drug addict and alcoholic. In the last two years of my alcohol addiction, I was drinking a gallon of cheap vodka daily and barely eating. I would wake up with alcohol poisoning and often find myself in the bathroom vomiting. It became a ritual. I would make it through the morning just waiting to get to the time when I could have my first drink again.

My alcoholism was so extreme that I reached a point where I thought I was having a heart attack. After going to a doctor, he told me I was having delirium tremors and my body was shutting down. He said, "Son, you've only got one drink left." This was a pivotal point in my life. It was either break though or die. I don't recommend you break through this way. You don't have to wait until your back is against the wall to change.

That day I chose life. I checked into a county detox program in Stockton, California. This place was no Passages in Malibu. It wasn't the Betty Ford Clinic. This was a state-run detox center for drug addicts and alcoholics. It's the place where I chose to commit to changing how I was living and being.

I've overcome a lot in my life. Many times I found myself going up the down staircase. Once again, I don't recommend you do things the way I did. I'm writing this book because I want to bestow the knowledge I've learned and experienced over a lifetime of overcoming physical and emotional addictions. I've gone from being incarcerated for driving while intoxicated and hitting three parked cars, all while transporting a quarter pound of cocaine, to becoming a millionaire in two different businesses. I also have twenty-plus years of experience as a success and addiction coach where I assist men and women who are seeking positive change. My goal is for you to make breakthroughs a way of life. To do this, you require a better understanding of why you do what you do so you can create the changes you are seeking.

I've had the privilege of seeing many of my clients over the years reinvent themselves and break through to new levels of consciousness and success. To date I've coached over twelve thousand clients—that's sixty thousand hours of personal one-on-one coaching during which I've been able to facilitate change. I walk my clients through the events that have shaped the feelings that have led to their addicted state.

Addictions are not just physical. Most addictions start as an emotional addiction. Prolonged feelings of guilt, shame, anger, hate, resentment, overwhelm, fear, abandonment, and rejection are the states of being that create addictions. The addictions I see most often are procrastination, perfectionism, disorganization, under-earning, chronic debiting, gambling, drugs, alcohol, bulimia, anorexia, overeating, codependence, and sex.

When you experience a breakthrough, you create "aha" moments, synchronicity, and synchro-destiny. Breaking through means that you decide, you commit, you understand, and you know. It's a "one day at a time" process. Your adversary typically is going to be your mindset. This is your emotionally addicted self that keeps you in a state of anger, hate, resentment, guilt, shame, abandonment, rejection, overwhelmed feelings, grief, and apathy. These emotions create anxiety, which results in the fight-or-flight response in your body.

Fight-or-flight is a physiological reaction that occurs in response to a perceived harmful event, attack, or threat to survival. It's a stress response that triggers the release of hormones to prepare your body to either fight and face the threat or flee to safety. This originated when our ancient ancestors were surrounded by predators and faced danger in their environment. This was their survival mechanism. Today, even though you are not in physical danger, your mind can trigger this response from thinking and feeling states of anxiety. This means you can trigger the response by simply thinking about situations that are imaginary, that haven't happened yet, or that have happened in the past.

For many people, living in fight-or-flight is a regular occurrence. It becomes a familiar state of anxiety and a familiar state of being. Fear, doubt, and overwhelmed states of being are what keep them avoiding success. They hold on to a set of feelings based on events from their life. And these events shape how they react, behave, and stay stuck. They stay in a state of not understanding why they are the way they are. They don't understand why they do what they do.

A large percent of society is unaware, overwhelmed, overweight, and unsure; they live in a repressed emotional state. If this is you and you seek to change, then breaking through would be your commitment. You cannot break through by merely being interested. You break through by being committed. For you to break through what is familiar, it's important that you understand why you do what you do. If you don't understand why you do what you do, you will continue to create the same identity, the same feelings, and the same emotions. You become emotionally addicted to the same set of familiar circumstances.

Breaking through is not "How do I?" Breaking through is "I am." Breaking through is:

"I'm breaking through the barriers."

"I'm breaking through the wall."

"I'm breaking through my stories."

"I'm breaking through that which I hold on to, and I commit to letting go."

In the breakthrough process, it's imperative that you commit one day at a time. When you can focus on one minute, one hour, and one day at a time, you won't get overwhelmed by the process.

Emotional Vibrational States

Energy is measured in cycles per second. The emotional scale coincides with the levels of consciousness. This ranges from 0-1,000, with shame being at the bottom of the scale and enlightenment being at the top. We all vibrate this subtle hertz frequency. When events happen in life, your emotions are triggered. Your emotions play a large role in your vibrational state. When you feel love, you vibrate and emit a much higher frequency than when you feel fear.

All levels below 200 are destructive of life in both the individual and society at large; all levels above 200 are constructive expressions of power. The decisive level of 200 is the fulcrum that divides the general areas of force and power.[1]

The lowest energy we transmute our feelings from is anxiety. Anxiety is what we hold on to based on events that have shaped our feelings. This is why so many people worry all the time. They are stuck in past events, and their body believes it is happening now. Emotions have a corresponding response. When you're in a state of fight-or-flight, holding on to these emotions, you are virtually holding on to past events that are repressed or misunderstood. This is what will keep you overwhelmed.

As we move further into the content of the breakthrough process, I will demonstrate how specific situations from your childhood, your teenage years, and your adulthood have shaped your actions and reactions. As you are able to separate your feelings from past events, you will start to step out of struggle.

Identifying Struggle

The definition of *struggle* is "to make forceful or violent efforts to get free of restraint or constriction." If you feel like you are struggling in life, there is a high probability you are living in resistance. For many people, struggle is a way of life. Struggle is an identity. Struggle is noble for many people. Many people wave the flag in the noble struggler's hit parade. They join the band of struggle. They seek other people to struggle with.

Struggle is a dark energy and feels very heavy. It takes a lot of effort, and it's exhausting. To identify why you struggle, start to take a look at why you do what you do. When you struggle, you are living in resistance. Ask yourself, "What am I resisting?" Resistance is force. You cannot force yourself to succeed. You cannot force yourself to break through. In force, you are in a state of suffering.

One of my clients had been in a state of struggle with her health. She struggled with back pain that resulted in a spinal fusion surgery. A year later she had to have a second back surgery because the first one had failed. Soon after she developed gut issues. For eight years of her life, she lived in struggle. And then one day, she had a breakthrough. She uncovered the mind-body connection to the stuffed emotions keeping her stuck. She made a decision to no longer live in force—to no longer live in the past. She let go and let God. She made a commitment to no longer embrace the struggle. It took one decision for her health to rapidly improve.

When you become enlightened, you no longer struggle. This is when you begin breaking through the nonphysical emotional state of anxiety. You step into a state of conscious awareness where you "know." In a "know state," you don't doubt. When you doubt, you struggle with your decisions, your commitments, and your ideas. You become indecisive, and this is how you overwhelm yourself. Procrastination sets in, and you continually get ready to get ready.

In this state of unconscious, subconscious, un-awareness, you use a communication style that sounds like this:

"I don't know."

"I don't know why I do this."

"I don't know why I struggle."

"I don't know why I struggle with dieting."

"I don't know why I drank last night."

In an "I don't know" state, you're in denial.

When you're committed and no longer attached to the mind-body connection to the events that shaped your struggle, you can let go of struggle. You're no longer marching in the struggler's hit parade. You're no longer the bandleader, the major, the majorette. You're able to step into a state of emotionally aware consciousness. You begin to live in love, joy, bliss, prosperity, and reciprocity. You no longer relapse. Cheating is no longer an option. You become rigorously honest with yourself and with others. When you let go of struggle, your emotional etheric energy begins to shift. There is a different level of alignment.

Struggling is connected to avoiding and procrastinating. When you struggle with a decision or struggle with commitment, you're giving yourself permission to avoid and procrastinate. *Procrastination* comes from the Latin word *procrastinare*, meaning "to avoid." When you're a chronic avoider, you're also a starter and typically not a finisher. Many people struggle with commitment. It is unequivocally one of the biggest struggles that a large percent of the world populace battles with. For many people, struggle is their identity.

Struggle has a lot of moving parts. You start off the

day wrong. You don't make your bed. You spend most of the day being overwhelmed. You're chronically late. You're unorganized. You're undisciplined. The bills mount up. The clutter mounts up. You're struggling with how to start, how to finish, what to do, and who to be.

Struggle leads to the emotion called overwhelm. If you're overwhelmed, it means you have a lot going on in your mind. The noise in your head is loud. You're indecisive. You have a lot of obligations that you've over-obligated yourself to completing. You do more for others than you'd ever do for yourself, and you struggle to break through. You struggle with breaking free. This is what many noble strugglers do. They hold on.

Many of my clients ask me how to let go of struggle. It's not asking, "How do I let go of struggle?" Struggle requires a state of awareness where you begin to understand why you do what you do. To begin releasing struggle consciousness, start by uncovering why you struggle.

Answer the Following Questions:

- Are you clear on your dreams and goals or are you uncertain?
- Do you prioritize your tasks?
- Do you over-obligate yourself to others to gain love and approval?
- Are you disorganized?
- Do you procrastinate or are you productive?
- Do you blame others for your challenges?
- Do you hold your parents, a business partner,

or an ex-spouse responsible for your struggles?
- What situations or actions do you keep repeating in your life?

By asking yourself these types of questions, you can begin to uncover the cause creating the effect of struggle in your life. As you begin to move into a state of power and let go of force, you change the neurochemical response in your brain that keeps you holding on to an emotionally addicted state, that keeps you in anxiety. When you understand how you have been running on autopilot, you can put your hands on the controls and begin to navigate in a new direction.

Disempowering Habits and Language

We all are creatures of habit. The question is, are your habits empowering you or disempowering you? Take a look at how your habits affect you. If your habits keep you in an emotional state where you feel guilty, shameful, and disappointed, to break through you would have to begin by recognizing this correlation. Your habits are a direct reflection of why you struggle.

When you have disempowering habits, you'll have challenges managing moving parts in life because you're overwhelmed. If you grow up with parents or people in your circle of influence that are rigid, neurotic, and no matter what you do it's never good enough, there's a high probability you'll rebel, especially rebelling against yourself. Rebelling against yourself is not conducive to creating outcomes that are favorable.

One of the first habits to begin with is making your bed. When you start to make your bed, even though making your bed seems so mundane, you can begin to wire your brain with habits that empower you. Making your bed is the first task you should accomplish in the morning. So much of society avoids the simple act of pride, dignity, and a task well done when it comes to making their bed because they rebel against it. Admiral William H. McRaven gave a commencement address at University of Texas at Austin in 2014 and spoke about this very topic.

> If you make your bed every morning you will have accomplished the first task of the day. It will give you a small sense of pride, and it will encourage you to do another task and another and another. By the end of the day, that one task completed will have turned into many tasks completed. Making your bed will also reinforce the fact that little things in life matter. If you can't do the little things right, you will never do the big things right.

Changing your habits is a "one day at a time" process. All of your habits are not likely to change overnight, but you can begin with a few simple disciplines that you begin to do daily. With repetition and experience, you will begin to see the compounded effect of your new habits.

Your disempowering habits are fostered by disempowering language. The two go together. Language creates action. Inaction creates inactivity. If you're not taking action, you're rebelling against the result because you're not sure if you can control the outcome. If that's you, these are habits that no longer serve you. Even though you may know and understand that, you have to implement the emotional skills to let go of the cause that creates the effect of why you do what you do. This is what creates an attractor factor conducive to an outcome that is empowering.

When you have disempowering language, you'll use words like "guess" mid-sentence. You'll say "need to" over and over. *Need* is a word of noncommitment. It's one of the most commonly used words in the English language that embraces and edifies not committing.

"I need to go to the store."

"I need to change."

"What I need to do . . ."

"I need to do this."

"I need it now."

Need is a word that the American populace uses to perpetuate a state of noncommitment. If you're commitment-phobic, you'll have challenges being decisive.

A large percent of the population takes the phrase

"kind of" and turns it into "kinda." "Sort of" turns into "sorta." Even though those two words hooked together form one word, they have little to no meaning. They are words of noncommitment. When you speak in riddles in an overwhelmed state, when you speak in a noncommitted communication style, you'll attract to your reality the people and situations to fulfill the feelings of rejection and abandonment.

As you're able to easily and effortlessly let go by taking a deep breath, you will drop down in your lower abdomen and feel the release. That release creates an emotional state of awareness for about eight to fifteen seconds. This allows you to be present. You're here. You're now. There's no significance to the future and no regret from the past. You're able to communicate differently with yourself and others.

As you put the effort forth the effort to become the person you are capable of becoming, you will start to speak a language of empowerment, a language of commitment, and a language of decision. This is a state of consciousness that you be and stay in for the rest of your life.

On the other hand, if you're chronically late, chronically overwhelmed, worried all the time, if your language style isn't conducive to being in a state of flow, then you'll live in resistance. When you're overwhelmed, you'll be unorganized. When you're unorganized, you have a lot of clutter. Then you'll get behind. You won't be able to manage the moving parts in your life because you're too overwhelmed.

"I don't know where to start."

"I don't know where to begin."

"How do I? How do I? How do I?"

"Would someone please tell me the rules."

"If someone would just show me the blueprint."

"If someone would tell me what to do, I'll do it."

It's not what you *do*. It's who you BE. You be in a state of recovery. You start to change your behaviors that create your habits. You begin to have emotional discipline. Discipline takes on a different context in recovery. Discipline doesn't mean that someone is going to discipline you or discipline is hard. Discipline means you become a disciple—a disciple of success, a disciple of recovery.

Stepping into Recovery

When you are in recovery, there are no more cheat days. You let go of your disempowering habits. You don't wait to the last minute to do your laundry. You don't do your laundry when you're out of clothes. You don't wait until the last minute to file extensions to pay your taxes. You live in a routine, a structure, a method, and a system. You begin to feel and be empowered. This happens when you let go of being disorganized and step into an organized state of consciousness. As you begin to have clarity about the outcome you seek, you no longer doubt yourself. You live in a state called aware. In your aware state, you know that you can finish what you start.

Many chronic strugglers start but don't finish. They're overwhelmed in anxiety, struggling to let go. Letting go is the ability to separate feelings from events. When you're not the mind-body connection to the events, then the events that shaped your feelings no longer have power. You don't live in a disempowered habitual state that leads to disappointment.

When you begin to understand how frequently you get disappointed and when you understand how many times you over-obligate yourself, then you can move into a state of awareness that can lead to recovery. But you can't recover by avoiding.

Recovery requires a commitment. It requires a "one day at a time" process where you commit to break through the conditioned behaviors that keep you doing what disempowers you and keeps you overwhelmed. When you let your body run your brain, you are running old programs based on events that have shaped your feelings.

To understand this more clearly, consider the following scenarios:

- Did you grow up in violence or dysfunction?
- Did you grow up in overwhelm?
- Did you grow up in a single-family home?
- Did you grow up with addiction in your home?
- Did you grow up with critical parents,

grandparents, or people in your circle of influence?

- Did you get picked on, traumatized, violated, molested, sexually abused, physically abused, or singled out by a series of bullies?

When you grow up in any of these types of situations, your body creates fight-or-flight. The emotions you experience create a corresponding response. Overwhelm sets in, and you start to hold your feelings in. You repress them and then your communication style is not conducive to creating favorable outcomes. You will attract and create the very situation you seek to avoid.

In order to create a new repetition and experience for an emotional state that will lead to a breakthrough, you have a better understanding of why you do what you. This opens the door so you can release and let go. You can begin to be and stay in a relaxed body one day at a time.

Ask Yourself

1. What are my top three areas of struggle?

2. What disempowering habits am I currently exhibiting? What new habits could I replace them with?

3. What old programs am I running based on past events? How do these programs affect me in my daily life?

FOR COMPANION RESOURCES, GO TO
https://goldenmastermind.com/breakthrough-factor
VIDEO: Identifying Change

TWO

YOUR STORY AND YOUR FAMILY'S STORY

Your story and your family's story constitute your history. We all go through a series of events in our lives that have led us to where we are today. Some of us grew up in a happy home, but many of us grew up with some form of dysfunction. Maybe we grew up with divorced parents, or with a family member or relative who struggled with addiction. We might have endured verbal, physical, or sexual abuse. Many of us were exposed to passive-aggressive personalities. A parent may have abandoned us, or we had to take on an adult role as a child.

The events in your life shape your feelings. They shape your moods and your behaviors. How does your story and your family's story affect you today? How does it affect you on a daily basis? How do you limit yourself based on past events? These are all great questions to ask yourself when you are committed to breaking through. Often we walk through life looking through the dirty lens of our past when all we have to do is get out the glass cleaner and wipe away what no longer serves us.

To break through, you have to begin letting go of

your old story. In the breakthrough process, your old story no longer serves you. It's the story that says:

"I'm not worthy."

"I don't deserve it."

"I'm not good enough."

"I grew up on the wrong side of the tracks."

"I've been abandoned, neglected, abused, traumatized, left behind."

"I'm waiting for my father to pick me up, but he doesn't show up."

Yes. That story.

Have you suffered enough? Have you been through enough? Are you tired of carrying the noble struggler flag? Are you tired of dragging around the ten-foot grandfather clock that's been strapped to your wrist for the last twenty-five years? If you're tired of your story, then it's absolutely time to let go of it.

To let go of your story, you learn to address these statements:

"I don't know."

"My childhood was like a blur."

"I don't know why I process."

"I don't know why I procrastinate."

"I don't know why I get ready to get ready."

"I don't know why I'm late all the time."

"I don't know why I get going and then seem to crash."

In this state of mind, you will stay addicted to denial.

A lot of people are addicted to being addicted. Being addicted becomes a way of life. When you are addicted, you will attract people and situations to your reality to fulfill a biochemical craving.

When you are in this state consistently, the payoff results in gaining pleasure from suffering. I know it sounds contradictory, but this is what happens to many people. There is a sense of satisfaction from being let down once again. Then you can say, "I knew this would happen" or "This always happens to me." You become addicted to negative events and experiences. You stay stuck in your story, proving to yourself that you don't deserve to break through.

Many of us, myself included, have put ourselves in the wrong places. People who care about us may have put us in the wrong places. Because we were in the wrong places, we became victims of traumatic situations. These events began the cycle of disappointment. To break the cycle, you begin by letting go of perpetrators and people that mistreated you. This is the power of forgiveness, which I will discuss in further detail later in the content of this book. To be clear, when you forgive, you are not letting the violator off the hook for what they did to you. What you are doing is no longer letting the events define you.

What you go through creates your character; that's the courage, the guts, the intestinal fortitude. When you can let go of the emotional attachment to your story, you will be able to tell the facts of your story without getting emotional. That's when you are overcoming your story. That's when you are breaking through.

Here are some of the facts of my story. Three years into my sobriety, in 1990, I was fresh off the streets of addiction. I had shoulder-length hair. I was a rebel without a cause. Network marketing found me, and by God I thought I was going to tear it up. I didn't. I was seduced into leasing an office in Dublin, California. I signed a $4,000-a-month lease for a year. The only way for me to cover the cost was to rent desk space to my teammates.

At this time in my life, I was very negative, very aggressive, and way too intense for my own good. What eventually happened was that my teammates cornered me in my cubicle and threw down on me verbally. They let me know they were going to abandon the office with the lease in my name. That would have meant bankruptcy for me. They gave me a seven-day period to grow up.

They then used a sage smudge stick to rid the space (and me) of negative energy. Sage has a distinct smell that closely resembles marijuana. Shortly after, the fire department arrived. They showed up at the office because my neighbors were complaining of the smell. The smoke had traveled into the ventilating system. Even after the explanation, I was still evicted.

I received a great lesson from my teammates. This was a turning point where I was given the opportunity to change my story. I humbled myself and apologized to people. I made amends. In your life as well, there will be events that offer you the opportunity to either break through or break down. It is your choice to change.

The number one reason that people don't reinvent themselves and create a new story is they are not patient enough. They expect to be successful without going through the process or putting in the effort. If they don't succeed in the first ninety days, six months, or two years, they quit. They say things like, "It didn't happen." "It didn't work for me." "I didn't succeed." Their commitment was not in alignment with their body. This is a recipe for disappointment.

As you have a better understanding of your story, your history, and the events that shape your feelings, you can separate yourself from those events. As a result, the events no longer create a neurochemical response that keep you emotionally overwhelmed. When you are committed, decisive, and ready to let go, letting go becomes an asset. It becomes an experience. It becomes a way of life. When you live in a place called ease, what you do is easy and effortless. When you focus on results and solutions, you're no longer the mind-body connection that kept you in an anxious, overwhelmed state.

In my one-on-one coaching of over 60,000 hours, over 12,000 clients, and over twenty-one-plus years of being a personal success coach, mentor, and assisting people with their recovery, I have found that a large percentage of the population stays in a repressed state. The medical community diagnoses it as a depressed state. In reality there are many repressed feelings that people hold on to. As Dr. Neel Burton says in a *Psychology Today* article:

> Although repressed material is unconscious, it is no less present and can (and usually does) resurface in strange and disturbing forms. The inability to process and come to terms with repressed material can lead to a lack of insight and understanding—as, for example, in the case of the person who thinks that his abusive father is a gentle and loving man. But it can also lead to a range of psychological problems such as difficulty concentrating, irritability, anxiety, insomnia, nightmares, and depression, and to maladaptive and destructive patterns of behavior such as anger and aggression in the face of reminders of the repressed material.[2]

When you don't know why you do what you do, there's a high probability that you have forgotten the events from your past that have shaped your behaviors. You may tell yourself you don't remember. This happens so you don't have to feel the emotional pain. If you are experiencing an effect in your life and you are committed to changing, you require uncovering the cause.

Cause and Effect

If you're able to chronologically go back through your history, you will have a better understanding of why you do what you do. It's very common for clients of mine to tell me that their whole childhood was a blur. By asking them some simple questions, their memory begins to return. Here are some of the questions I ask:

- Who was your third grade teacher?
- Can you name one person who was in your kindergarten class?
- Where did you go to grade school?
- Do remember any activities or sports you played at recess?

Through these questions, I begin breaking down the cause that creates the effect for my clients so they can break through. You can do the same for yourself. When you understand why you do what you do, you have the opportunity to interrupt a feeling in mid-moment. You have the opportunity to create change.

Many people wait until the pain is great enough to change. That can be rock bottom, it can be rock middle, or it can be now. How strong is your desire to change?

Until you make the decision, you will perpetuate the same situations. You will hold on to the feelings that serve you. Yes, I said serve you, even though you tell yourself they don't serve you. They do serve you because your emotions create a corresponding response. You have become addicted to the release of neurochemicals. This emotional state forms your identity. It's why people find change challenging. When you change, you are creating a new identity.

When you are committed one day at a time to changing, you start to develop a new brain. When you hold on your current feelings, you continue to stay in a wired brain that keeps you repeating the same situation over and over. As you have a better understanding of the events that have shaped your feelings, you can separate your feelings from the events. Your feelings about the events are what created the effects.

When you worry all the time, that is an effect. When you're overwhelmed frequently, that is an effect. When you are always late, that is an effect. When you smoke cigarettes to address your stress, that is an effect. Smoking is not a cause, yet that is what people attempt to address. They wear a patch, they get hypnosis, they chew gum—they address the behavior instead of the cause of the behavior. If you chronically relapse on food to fulfill feelings that you suppress and repress, that is an effect. The events that have shaped your feelings are the true cause of your behaviors.

Somewhere between five and fifteen years old, a large percentage of your identity is formed through the circle of influence you grow up with. If you get picked on the playground, traumatized in your household, that has an effect on you. On the other end of the spectrum, if you are loved by your family, that also has an effect. Whether you are given nurturing and support or you are criticized frequently, these events shape your identity.

The Events

Your negative feelings about the events you experience create low self-esteem. This is why you end up feeling dependent upon recognition, rewards, someone else's approval, and someone else's love to feel good about yourself. You exist in a state of dependence based on the events and how you were conditioned to behave.

> Layer by layer, we wear various emotions, which form our identity. In order to remember who we think we are, we have to recreate the same experiences to reaffirm our personality and the corresponding emotions. As an identity, we become attached to our external world by identifying with everyone and everything, in order to remind us of how we want to project ourselves to the world.[3]

If you are stuck in a story that doesn't serve you, it's time to change your perception of the events. Every time your replay the events in your mind, your body believes it is reliving the event. It relives the emotional state of the event. This is how emotional addiction begins.

The events have significance to you, but the amount of significance you give an event determines whether you become a victim or a victor. That's why it is so important to be objective about the events.

We all have baggage from the past, but if you desire to break through, you will have to change the lens through which you view the events. An event is an event. It is your thoughts about the event that give it meaning. The goal is to neutralize the story you tell yourself.

If you were abused, you may tell yourself you are not lovable. You may tell yourself that you are damaged goods. You may think you don't deserve better. Breaking through requires releasing the negative meaning you have given to the abuse. The abuse was an event, just like lightning striking a tree is an event. The tree is not bad or unworthy because lightning struck it. Yes, the event happened, but it does not define who you are at your core. Your thoughts about the past are what keep it alive in the present moment.

When you don't understand how events have shaped your feelings and behaviors, you will become a willing participant in other people's conflict. This happens when you encounter passive-aggressive personalities. You become their counterforce and a source of conflict. As a result, this fulfills your low self-esteem and disappointment. Often these types of people show up in your life based on your law of attraction. This occurrence fulfills your feelings based on past events. This is why you will hear people say, "I married my mother," or "I married my father."

They married a person who fulfills their feelings from childhood conditioning as they grew up.

Conditioned Behavior

When you begin to let go of the conditioned behavior that keeps you doing the same thing over and over, you no longer experience the mind-body connection to the events that shaped your anxiety.

Your conditioned behavior is based on the ideas you have formed from the events in your life. If you did not feel safe in your childhood, you are likely to be mistrusting of people now. If you had strict rules to follow as a child, you may become a people pleaser as an adult. If you grew up with addiction in your home or had to take on an adult role as child, it is very likely that you will develop codependent tendencies. These are examples of the cause-and-effect relationships based on past events.

Doubt is another conditioned emotional state. If you grew up with a narcissistic parent, it's easy to internalize feelings of not being good enough. This happens because you frequently felt that you were wrong. Doubting yourself becomes a state of being. Doubt prevents you from breaking through.

Events are what shape and condition your feelings of rejection, abandonment, anger, guilt, worry, and all the other low vibrational emotional states. Here is an example. If you grew up with a parent that was an alcoholic or drug addict, it likely means you grew up in unpredictability. You never knew what kind of mood your parent was going to be in. You may have been slapped for making too much noise or coming down the stairs at the wrong time. One minute your parent is telling you they love you, and the next they are angry and throwing things.

This is how getting in trouble can become a way of life. It is why so many people check out or become processors. They try not to get in trouble. They are conditioned to be people pleasers.

Processing and Checking Out

You do not process because you're a processor. You do not analyze because you are an analyzer. You do not think because you are a thinker, and you do not check out because you have checked out. You do this because it is a conditioned behavior.

Being checked out means that rather than being and staying attentive, you tell yourself you have to move on. You tell yourself you don't know the answer. A person who checks out typically talks in long riddles. They speak in long, slow statements. They don't answer questions.

Why does this happen? If you grew up with passive-aggressive people in your circle of influence, it most likely was common for you to be put in a position where you had to explain, validate, and justify your existence.

But what does checking out actually mean? My own interpretation is that you tend to go into your analyzing mind to resolve the problem. If you grew up in a situation where you might get in trouble, be invalidated, judged, or criticized, it is common to become overly careful in your communication style. It is common to use *umm, uh-huh, well, okay* and create a sense of uncertainty when you speak. This way of speaking keeps you safe, but it also keeps you procrastinating.

Part of your left brain's process is to resolve problems. If you perceive a situation to be painful, your left brain will do what it is conditioned to do. It will teach you to avoid the perceived pain. This is why people avoid success yet tell themselves they're avoiding failure. They use the anxiety of rejection and abandonment as one of their key procrastination techniques so as not to engage in change. By not failing, they stay disappointed.

As you begin to understand your story, your family's story, and the events from your past, you will enter a new state of awareness. This is where you begin to be in your power. You are able to look at a situation objectively. You are able to see a situation for what it is. You do not give meaning to events from your past. As you begin to get honest, tell the truth, and understand the facts of your past, you can let go of the events that have shaped your feelings.

Repression

Repression happens when you hold on to events that shape your feelings. Negative emotions—typically guilt, shame, abandonment, grief, rejection, anger, and resentment—are stored in the body without you consciously knowing they are there. When you don't have a memory of these emotions and you are unable to release them, they will remain repressed or suppressed.

When I initially ask my coaching clients why they do what they do, I receive a lot of, "Huh, I don't know." "I'm not sure." "I had a good childhood." "I don't understand." "I don't remember." If you hold on to events that shape your feelings, you'll repress your feelings, telling yourself, "I don't remember my childhood." "My whole childhood was a blur." "Up until age eleven, I have no memory."

This is a state of consciousness is called denial, meaning that a large percent of what happened to you between zero and seven years old remains repressed. Those events are in a lockbox. You don't want to know because you tell yourself you don't want to feel the pain. The reality of the situation is that when you're no longer the mind-body connection to the body of pain you continue to perpetuate, then you will be pain-free.

Instead of living with a sinus migraine headache, you become clear and understand why you do what you do. The mind-body connection to a sinus headache is usually related to someone close to you. You feel irritated due to someone creating stress, sadness, or anger. As you let go of the symptoms and start to address the cause, you can let go of the ailment and change the way you feel about yourself.

When you're in a deep process of recovery, you will start to scale up the emotional scale of energy. You'll start to live in an aware state, loving who you're becoming. And as you move into this level of higher vibration, you'll start to live in a place called joy and bliss. This is where you'll begin to attract your reality, events, people, situations, and opportunities that will fulfill your dreams, purposes, goals, and objectives. This state of being is where your attractor factor begins to change.

In the mid-nineties, this happened to me. I was a $100,000 in debt. Due to some poor choices, mismanaged credit, being overwhelmed, and being in two companies that went out of business back-to-back, I was left holding the bag on a large amount of unsecured credit card debt. I had reached an emotional and financial rock bottom. The situation had to change. I had been struggling for a number of years and didn't understand what breakthroughs meant.

I had ten years of sobriety at that time, but I was still a very resentful, angry addict. My anger wasn't as covert as it was repressed, and I felt I could fake myself through it when in reality I was very uncomfortable in this state. So uncomfortable that my body began to react to the stimulus I was creating. I developed migraine headaches and was grinding my teeth.

When I got clear and began to break through and had a better understanding of why I did what I did, I began to reflect in rigorous honesty without justifying or criticizing myself. When I had a better understanding of why I did what I did, I was able to separate my feelings from the events. My energy began to shift. I became the most focused I'd ever been. I was in a relaxed yet intense state called production. I wasn't neurotic about production. I was committed to production and committed to results. I knew that the only way out of the situation I had created was to out produce my problems.

In reality, you don't want to create problems. You want to create results. But if you've created problems, you want to tell yourself:

"This is the end of the era."

"This is the death of the anxious ego."

"There will be no more cheat days as of today."

"I'm using empowering language and
affirmations to foster my purpose."

"I'm no longer the mind-body connection."

"I'm the leader that people are looking for."

There's no time stamp on change. Change is now. Change is when you're ready. Change is when you are ready to let go of the cause that creates the effect of what you hold onto. Changing is not "How do I change?" Change is "I am changing." When you separate your feelings from the past, you're able to let go of why you do what you do.

Ask Yourself

1. What is my chronology? Make a timeline of events that you believe contribute to your story.
2. What conditioned behaviors have shaped my behavior today?
3. What correlations do I see between the events from my past and the effects in my present?

FOR COMPANION RESOURCES, GO TO
https://goldenmastermind.com/breakthrough-factor
PODCAST: Jeffery Combs Interviews
Dr. Joe Dispenza, DC
VIDEO PODCAST: Why You Do What You Do

THREE

ADDICTIONS

What is an addiction? An addiction is the physical or emotional drive for a substance. That substance can be a drug, or it can be the neurochemicals released from an emotional state. Over time the body craves more because it reaches an addiction tolerance. An addict always wants a little bit more, which is why larger doses are required.

Stress can trigger trauma. In order to not feel emotional pain, addiction often becomes the escape. The addiction is a way to avoid the pain. Addiction can also begin as conditioned behavior. Food addiction is one of the most common addictions that starts as a conditioned behavior in childhood. Since it's so readily accessible, food is often used as a drug of choice.

Why do we become addicts? In our brains, we have a set of neurons that fire and wire together based on familiar feelings. We become addicted to certain substances or activities so we can stuff a feeling. We are addicted to not have to experience pain. Oftentimes our past ends up being the anchor that drags us under, holds us down, and keeps us stuck. Much of the pain we experience can be physical, but a large percentage of it is emotional. This process is the way we can become hard-wired to be an addict.

The main addictions I see manifest in my clients are the following:

- procrastination
- drama and chaos
- overeating/under-eating
- being overwhelmed
- illegal drugs and pharmaceutical medication
- alcohol

These then branch off to all the other addictions:

- compulsive spending
- compulsive gambling
- compulsive debting
- compulsive sex
- compulsive compulsiveness
- disappointment
- conflict
- neurotic behavior

Most of my clients do not understand their addictions when we start coaching. I teach them that addiction is what keeps them living in an energetic state of low vibration. It is a state of force and a state of dis-ease in the body. David Hawkins explains it this way:

The ways the various levels of human consciousness express themselves are profound and far-reaching; their effects are both gross and subtle. All levels below 200 are destructive of life in both the individual and society at large; all levels above 200 are constructive expressions of power. The decisive level of 200 is the fulcrum that divides the general areas of power and force.[4]

On an emotional scale of energetic vibration, level 200 is focused on personal survival. Below this level you will find vibrations coming from anxiety. When your level of emotional vibration comes from anxiety, which is anger, hate, resentment, guilt, shame, abandonment, rejection, and overwhelmed feelings, you transmute your feelings at the lowest levels of vibration. A low vibrational state is what hinders you in life, in business, and in entrepreneurship.

Consider this situation. If you smoke and hide your smoking, factor how much time it takes throughout the day to be an addict. How long does it take to smoke a cigarette? Five minutes. How about all the time and preparation that goes into it? What about planning how you are going to sneak out? Where you are going to smoke? Where you are going to buy the cigarettes? How you are going to wash your hands? What mouthwash will you use to gargle with? Think of the clothes you have to wash. You have to spray your clothes down before you go back inside. You have to get in your car to drive down the street—now you have to spray the car down. Before you even get back, you are exhausted. You are overwhelmed being an addict.

Until you step into recovery, you will be an active addict. To be able to let go of an addiction is to let go of the past. It means letting go of the events and letting go of the negative emotions.

I have many clients that are in sales. One of the most common challenges they encounter is that when they look at a telephone or a lead list, their neurons that fire and wire together start creating a way to avoid rejection.

But it's not about rejection. It's about past events when they were judged. It's about about feelings that are not serving them. It's about being criticized. It's about being called on the carpet. It's about having to validate, explain, and justify themselves.

When you understand why you do what you do, you have the opportunity, through consciousness and awareness, to be able to let go. You cannot let go when you are in denial. When you focus on addressing the effect of your addiction, you will overlook the cause. You cannot let go of the ghost from your past if you do not know the ghost. You will hear me say this many times throughout this book: to break through, you must begin to understand the cause that creates the effect.

Addiction Tolerance

Over time you will begin to build up an addiction tolerance to your drug of choice. When I say drug, I mean whatever it is that gives you an emotional high or low. This can be a physical drug, but it can also be the neurochemicals released when you eat a candy bar or when you become angry or disappointed. The tolerance happens when you no longer respond to a drug the way you did the first time you experienced it. You crave a little more to get the same effect.

Addiction tolerance is created over a long period of time. When you are emotionally addicted to a set of events from your past, your body begins to crave and recreate situations to fulfill the feelings from your past. As you encounter similar situations that bring up feelings of abandonment, guilt, shame, rejection, anger, and other low vibrational emotional energies, your tolerance increases. When you have a better understanding of why you do what you do, you can begin to interrupt yourself mid-moment and mid-feeling to break the cycle.

If you have a high tolerance to being an addict, then it is likely you have been an emotional addict for a large percentage of your life. The following list provides indications you may have built up an emotional addiction tolerance.

- If you were overwhelmed as a child and you're still overwhelmed today
- If you are a chronic co-dependent, over-obligating, enabling, doing more for others and putting yourself last
- If you find yourself angry frequently
- If you are constantly in conflict
- If you do not understand why people are always picking on you

- If you brood and pout
- If you check out and process
- If you have an unorganized and undisciplined mindset
- If you have challenges getting and staying organized
- If you are chronically late

Many of the stories you tell yourself are by-products of the events that shaped your feelings from childhood. When you were never good enough growing up, you are likely still operating from that "I'm never good enough" state as an adult.

In the breakthough process, you have to ask yourself, "Have I suffered enough?" "Am I a noble struggler?" If the answer is yes, then step out of your victim mentality.

Stop avoiding transformation and step into your power. Rise to the occasion and allow yourself to be the person you know you're capable becoming one day at a time. As you let go of your addiction tolerance, your objective is to separate your feelings from events. When you are committed to letting go, part of the process is letting go of the limiting beliefs that you perpetuate to be and stay disappointed.

Limiting Beliefs

Your beliefs are a direct reflection of events and situations that have happened in your life. It is not only the events that shape your beliefs but your perception of the beliefs. It is your thoughts that rule your actions.

Your actions either create a feeling of positivity or a feeling of negativity. If you have limiting beliefs, they will limit your ability to succeed.

Limiting beliefs can stem from feelings of guilt and shame or other low levels of consciousness based on past events. These beliefs lead to not feeling good enough, not feeling capable enough, and not feeling smart enough. You may feel you will be judged and criticized. Events and your perception of the events shape your beliefs and create your sense of certainty or uncertainty.

I've asked this question many times: "If you are absolutely, unequivocally certain that you would succeed, what would you do?" And in reply I hear, "I'd give it my best effort. I would do whatever I had to do." Your best effort, one day at a time, over a period of time is what will create the action required to succeed. But worrying about the outcome, judging yourself, and turning on the critical advisor will keep you in a state of inaction. By not taking action, you stay in a place that keeps you safe from failing, but it also keeps you disappointed because you are not succeeding. This thought process is contradictory, and it's due to your limiting beliefs.

Many people's beliefs about money keep them from ever being able to attract or create wealth. That is why people tend to have more liabilities than assets. Their dialogue with money is not conducive to attracting money itself or attracting the people they can create it with.

Your dialogue with money is a direct reflection of

your beliefs. If you believe money is difficult, money is scarce, money is hard to find, money does not grow on trees, or if you believe that you grew up on the wrong side of the tracks, you are using a series of disempowering statements that separate you from the opportunity to create wealth. You are separating yourself from the opportunity to attract money and attract people to collaborate with. This is how you contradict living in prosperity.

Living in indecision and poverty consciousness is a direct reflection of the way you have been conditioned to behave in relation to money. By the time you are eighteen years old, most of your beliefs about money have been established by the twenty thousand meals you have spent with people in your circle of influence. If you desire to break through, then it is time to change your philosophy.

If you keep doing what you are doing and it keeps getting you what you are getting, isn't it time to take a good look and have a better understanding of the cause that creates the effect? When you recognize that you have not developed the correct mindset yet, you now have the awareness to create change. You can begin to develop the mindset, the skills, and habits to move into the law of alignment.

 To move out of the addicted brain, the most important beliefs to develop are that you are enough; you are lovable. That is the fundamental foundation. You have to be able to say, "I am enough. I'm lovable. I'm capable. I can be it. I can do it." That type of belief doesn't limit you. Instead it attracts a whole different type of person and situation to your reality. That vibration is much higher than anxiety or doubt. When you begin to live in love, joy, bliss, and enlightenment, you will attract a whole different situation to your reality.

Addiction keeps you in a state of disbelief. So, when do you change? When the pain is great enough. You will have to determine when that is. But when the pain is great enough can be right here and right now. It means you have suffered enough. You understand that being a noble struggler will never take you to the land of paradise. As you begin to let go and no longer be the mind-body connection to the events that have shaped your feelings, you are letting go of beliefs that do not serve you.

Ask Yourself

1. What physical and/or emotional addictions do I have challenges with?
2. What are the main events from my past that have led to my addictive behavior?
3. What limiting beliefs are holding me back from breaking the addictive cycle? What new beliefs would I have to accept to break through?

FOR COMPANION RESOURCES, GO TO
https://goldenmastermind.com/breakthrough-factor
VIDEO: Identifying Your Addiction
PODCAST: Jeffery Combs Interviews John Assaraf
PODCAST: 7 Effects of Growing Up in an Addicted

Home: Reconditioning Your Behavior for
Empowerment
BLOG ARTICLE: [Quiz] What's Your Level of
Procrastination?

FOUR

THE SCIENCE OF ATTRACTION

You may have heard of the law of attraction. This law teaches that through levels of consciousness we attract to our reality people and situations that fulfill our feelings. A simple definition is "like attracts like." Understanding and working with this law is what will foster your purposes, goals, dreams, and aspirations.

Levels of Consciousness

Levels of consciousness are calibrated on a scale from 0-1,200 in a logarithmic progression. This means that when you raise your consciousness a few points, you are making an exponential gain. The breakthrough factor starts to become a reality as you increase your level of consciousness.[5]

According to David Hawkins, MD, PhD, 78 percent of humanity calibrates below the consciousness level of 200. In America this figure is 49 percent.[6] This means that primitive instincts dominate most of the world. Level 200 is the fulcrum that divides power and force. As you begin to raise your level on the consciousness scale, you significantly increase your power to break through.

If you are currently operating at a very low level of energy, you will attract people and situations to fulfill the emotions in your current state of being. The main anxieties that affect your consciousness are anger, hate, resentment, guilt, shame, abandonment, rejection, overwhelm, grief, and apathy. When you spend a great deal of your time in fight-or-flight, in an overwhelmed body, you will attract to your reality people and situations that keep you anxious. This gives you little space to be conscious. To become consciously aware, you must separate your feelings from your anxiety. Anxieties are what keep you in an overwhelmed state.

Overwhelm leads to disorganization, being emotionally unavailable, being checked out, and doing the same thing repeatedly. You end up wondering why you don't get the prize, why you don't get the girl, why you don't get the man, why you don't get what you want. When you begin to have a better understanding of your anxieties, you can start to address the cause. That is where you enter the recovery process.

Living in levels of consciousness below 200 will keep you disappointed and chronically avoiding breaking through. You will continue to stay outside of success, hoping, wondering, wishing, and waiting for that mythical, magical moment to show up when you can cross the barrier to success. When you continue to stand behind the glass in anxiety, you do not have to perform.

Being in anxiety is an emotional addiction that keeps you under-earning, underachieving, underperforming, and most importantly, overwhelmed. When you live in anxiety, you're living in fight-or-flight. Your body secretes a series of neurochemicals that you become emotionally addicted to.

The lowest level of consciousness is when you are unconsciously doing the same thing over and over. When you stay in an emotional state of anxiety, you give yourself permission not to succeed—you don't have to be responsible for your success. When you are in anxiety, you can chronically avoid doing what you should do and instead stay disappointed.

Anxiety is closely followed by fear. Fear is a more physical presence. People fear flying; they're afraid the plane will crash. Fear often is synonymous with anxiety, but there is a distinct difference between the two. Anxiety is all about stories that have not yet happened. Fear is more about physical situations that could occur. Fear keeps you overwhelmed, much the way anxiety does. These levels of consciousness keep many people continuously getting ready to get ready.

Fear is often a misused word when it comes to understanding cause and effect. You don't fear success. You typically have anxiety about succeeding or anxiety about failing. To break through, you start to have a better understanding of why you have fear or why you are anxious.

The most common reason people have anxiety about success is that they have anxiety about change. Change means the end of the era, the death of the ego. As you have a better understanding of the stories you tell yourself and begin to separate your feelings from the stories, you can step into your power.

The lowest level of energy is shame and guilt. On the consciousness scale, it is somewhere between 20 to 40 cycles per second. The highest level of anxious energy is anger, hate, and resentment. In that type of energy, anger can fuel production. You can occasionally create results, but anger burns off quickly. It makes you unapproachable by the people you seek to have in your circle of influence.

As you begin to have a better understanding that your anger is usually a direct reflection of being emotionally, physically, or sexually violated, you then can start the recovery process. When you separate your feelings from the events that have happened, you raise your level of awareness. This is how you raise your consciousness. When you are consciously aware, you no longer experience the mind-body connection to the events that shaped your anxieties.

When you are in anxiety, you telepathically send a mixed message that says:

"Please join me, but I'm not good enough to lead you."

"I'd really like to succeed, but I'd rather live in doubt and play it safe." "I'd rather live in a low vibrational energy state, where it's safe—I don't have to be responsible, yet I'll stay disappointed."

The ultimate contradiction is when you seek success but fear it—when you are walking right up to success, but you walk around it because you are not sure if you can control the outcome. These are the emotions that keep you anxious.

A significant percentage of the population has deep emotional feelings about events they hold onto. They repress their feelings and keep themselves in an emotionally stuck state of overwhelm. Getting ready to get ready is the ultimate avoidance tendency that many people perpetuate.

A large percentage of the population spends a great deal of their time educating themselves. Their education becomes their medication. They continue to medicate themselves by getting educated. They have a whole shelf of self-help books. They go to seminars, rallies, conventions, and events. Events unequivocally can change your feelings and change your life. But unfortunately, many people go to events, and then the spray paint wears off the rust. The motivation from Saturday does not last until Wednesday. They go right back to getting ready to get ready in a chronic emotional state of anxiety.

When you have a better understanding and are consciously aware of the cause that creates the effect, you can practice the discipline of breathing, letting go, and releasing. This is how you change your consciousness. It's objectivity. It's metacognition. It's the ability to let go of the force you create that keeps you anxious. When you have a better understanding of why you do what you do and are able to separate your feelings from the events, you can begin the process of changing who and what you attract.

Power versus Force

You cannot make yourself break through. When you tell yourself you are going to force yourself or make yourself do something, it is likely not going to happen. You create resistance before you start. Living in force means you will require a counterforce. When you live in force, you attract perpetrators, violators, and passive-aggressive personalities that will put you in a position to validate, justify, and explain yourself.

When you stand in power, you no longer require a counterforce to fulfill your anxiety. Power stands alone. Power is an emotional discipline without any overwhelm. When you are in power, you do not emotionally relapse. There are no more cheat days. There is no more getting ready to get ready.

Power is nonlinear. It is not physical; it is emotional. When you are in a high level of consciousness, you are in power. You don't require any ulterior outside force to be in power because you can stand alone. You are no longer the mind-body connection to events that have shaped your addictions. Instead you live in a relaxed body. You have an emotional discipline that motivates you to make your bed in the morning. You don't rebel against yourself because you do not require a counterforce or an undertow to pull you back into doubt, fear, and anxiety.

In power, when you encounter passive-aggressive perpetrators, hostile people, or angry people who want to put you in a position to validate, justify, and explain yourself, you can neutralize your emotional state. You do not relapse into conflict, drama, and chaos. You do not overwhelm yourself with the possibilities of failing, being rejected, or making mistakes. You are self-actualized in the state of consciousness called production. When you can produce on command, you create results.

Many people focus on details that do not bring them results. They focus on not failing rather than on succeeding. A large percentage of the population continues to educate themselves to avoid success rather than teaching themselves to implement and integrate the content that will allow them to succeed. When you focus on not failing, you do not engage the habits, the mindset, and the skills of success.

Living in Force

If you grow up with passive-aggressive people in your circle of influence who hold you accountable for not being perfect and continuously criticize you, they become the force, and you play the role of their counterforce. Frequently, we mate, date, marry, and cohabitate with these people, who are often from our past. It fulfills our feelings of being overwhelmed and neurochemically addicted to a set of feelings that keep us feeling rejected and abandoned.

If you grew up with people who used guilt to

control you, you tend to become guilty, and then feel guilty all the time. When you grow up with people who are unpredictable, you worry about their unpredictability. Worrying all the time becomes your science of attraction.

When you hold on to events from the past, you magnetize, polarize, and attract to your reality people and situations to fulfill your feelings of anger, hate, resentment, guilt, shame, abandonment, rejection, overwhelmed feelings, grief, and apathy.

Chaos and Drama

It's important to understand how you or the people in your circle of influence become addicted to drama and chaos. A drama addict's ego continually attracts and creates drama, and it tends to weather the storms of crisis and chaos. Drama addicts tend to be responsible for the very drama that they create. They are addicted to their feelings, and they thrive on the adrenaline rush of saving the day under emergency conditions.

People addicted to drama can either be very meek and timid, or they can be hostile and energetic. Other people may have to constantly take care of the drama addict's personal and professional business while they pursue one distraction after another to keep their life dramatic and entertaining. This type of person will attract people and situations that will constantly send them into crisis mode.

If this is you and you live in drama and chaos, it

is likely that you will alienate other people because of your drama. On the flipside, you may have great people skills, so you can persuade people to rescue you. Drama addicts are very good at turning situations around so they can control other people's feelings, which then allows them to justify being a victim. It is one thing to have a challenging moment or two, but if you have frequent outbursts, blowups, meltdowns, or episodes of manipulation, it is likely that you are a drama addict. Your meltdown gives you a reason to stay in bed the next day. You have a reason to pull the covers up over your head to avoid reality. This is how you seduce family members or others in your circle of influence to rescue or take care of you.

To let go of your drama and chaos tendencies, you must develop an awareness about why you do what you do. When you know that it unequivocally no longer serves you, you can begin to break through. I went through this myself. I spent the last two years of my alcohol addiction in procrastination. I had a job, but I did just enough to get by. I barely made my quotas, yet I would drink myself into oblivion every single night.

Every day I would wake up with a hangover, and it would take a miraculous comeback early in the afternoon for the fog to lift. Then I would go into absolute overdrive and make up in the afternoon for what I did not do in the morning. At 5:00 p.m., my drinking bell would go off, and I'd repeat the pattern all over again.

If you have a lot of chaos in your life, it is absolutely

time to let go. Begin to objectively and realistically evaluate your situation. When you are trapped in self-destructive cycles of excitement and adrenaline rushes followed by collapses, you will never be able to appreciate the energizing value genuine peace of mind gives you. This is exactly what I have been learning for the last thirty years.

In recovery, I discovered that not only was I an addict, I was also very codependent. In other words, I could go into crisis mode, and I could also go into rescue mode. I could be a drama addict, and I could rescue drama addicts—either way, it fueled my self-esteem.

Codependency

Guilt is one of the biggest deterrents to creating success. Guilt is a heavy emotion that keeps you overwhelmed. When you are guilty all the time, you tend to over-obligate, do too much, and enable others so you can practice your codependency. When you are too guilty to let go, you use guilt as a deterrent to stay disappointed. You will over-obligate yourself and then feel resentful about the outcome because you did not get the recognition, the adoration, or the rewards you were seeking.

When you are codependent, you are not independent. In codependency, you require other people's personalities to fulfill your feelings because you require approval. You are worried about what other people think about you. You want to be able to control the outcome of others so you can control your feelings.

When you are codependent, you derive your personality from over-obligating, doing too much, serving, giving, and taking care of everyone but yourself. When you come last, everyone else comes first. If you become a rescuer, you give, give, give—and you are giving for approval. You end up disappointed that you are not recognized; you do not receive the love and appreciation you are seeking.

You want to be able to attract to your reality people you can collaborate and partner with; you want be part of a team, not deal with people who expect you to do everything for them. If you have to control other people's outcomes, it's exhausting. Codependent energy is draining. It will keep you feeling resentful because of all the time, money, and energy you pour into someone. You will resort to guilt to try and control the other person:

"Look at all I have done for you."

"Where is the gratitude?"

"Where is my thanks?"

"Why aren't you doing your part?"

You wonder why you are not getting the reward and

the payoff. Guilt has a cycle of resentment on the back end. When you operate out of guilt, you transmute energy at the lowest level you can send. You will attract people you can take care of who will disappoint you. When you live in this type of energy, you're going to live in an overwhelmed, disorganized state.

Disorganization

I believe the most challenging addiction to overcome is being disorganized. When you are disorganized, it shows up in many areas of your life. When you do not make your bed in the morning, you are rebelling against your success before you even start. Many people intellectualize this by saying, "Why would I make my bed when I'm going to get in it tonight?" The reason you make your bed is that it is the first discipline you start in your day. When you rebel against yourself the minute you get up, you rebel against yourself in many situations throughout the day.

When you are unorganized and undisciplined, you do not have a system by which to live. You are winging it. You are expecting to succeed by osmosis. You are hoping for life to hand you success on a silver platter. Unfortunately, it doesn't happen like that. When you wait for your ship to come in, you better find a rowboat because ships typically do not come in. The ship you are seeking requires that you build it by cutting down the lumber and putting sixteen penny nails in it. You are going to design this ship on *your* terms and *your* time frame. Then you will be able to take pride in the ship you've built that takes you to your dreams.

Dreaming is good, but you also have to take action toward those dreams. When you are disorganized and do not have a system, there is a high probability that you will never get around to living your dreams. You will stand on the outside of success waiting for that mythical moment when you are educated enough to organize yourself to be able to be successful.

Being disorganized is a mindset, just like being organized is a mindset. When you are organized, you have a system. People sometimes will accuse you of being OCD, neurotic, and unrealistic. If that's the case, consider the source. Typically unorganized people are the ones who are uncomfortable with your organization.

Many people are uncomfortable with their lack of success, so they project their uncomfortability on you about your success. It is imperative that you let these people go without feeling rejected, abandoned, and violated. Your objective is not to be the counterforce to someone else's force.

When someone asks you questions that put you on the spot, you want to recognize what is happening in the moment. Neutralize this personality by not giving them an explanation or sharing all the details or facts with them. You want to use questions to disarm them so you are not caught being the counterforce to someone else's force.

When you can stand in this kind of power, you do not require conflict, drama, or chaos to fulfill your disappointment. There are many drama and chaos addicts in the world, also called emotional and spiritual vampires. They derive their energy from taking it from you. These people use anger, hate, and resentment to provoke you. They also use force to put you into conflict with them. When you recognize this, you won't relapse into a set of familiar feelings based on past events from your childhood.

To break through, you must begin to address your disorganization and start to be organized—and stay organized—as you release the clutter and chaos from your life. When you begin to fill up the thirty-three-gallon heavy-duty garbage bags and start to live a more systematized, methodical, organized life, you will change your law of attraction.

When you are overwhelmed and undisciplined, you attract people similar to you to fulfill your feelings. You will have challenges being able to connect and collaborate with people who are systematic and organized based on how you feel about yourself. When you live in a low energetic vibrational state, you are relegated to having low self-esteem. You will not feel comfortable connecting with people who have influence and affluence. You will talk yourself into being rejected before it even happens as a way to fulfill your feelings.

When you understand that you are good enough and deserve to break through, you will not wing it to success or wing it to recovery. Recovery is a process focused on the principle of one day at a time. Success isn't so much about what you do. Success is about what you do *daily*. It's about who you are *being*. It is what you do daily that will compound. The repetition and experience are what will create autosuggestion.

When you commit to your recovery, it is imperative that one day at a time you master the simple emotional discipline that allows you to be organized instead of disorganized. When you start to organize your thoughts and feelings, you will be able to communicate clearly and effectively. You drop the mind-body connection to phrases such as:

"I don't know what to say."

"I don't know who to be."

"What am I supposed to do?"

"If somebody would just tell me what to do, I will."

As you gain command of your emotional state, you will be able to adapt and adjust. You will not hold on to the past to perpetuate a set of feelings to be disappointed.

Why We Hold On

Many people hold on to the past. They hold on to their feelings. Then when I ask them why they do what they do, I hear:

"I don't know."

"I'm not sure."

"I'm not certain."

In return, I reply, "If you did know, why do you do it?" When you don't know, you are holding on. You cannot break through if you are holding on to the past. Holding on to the past fulfills a set of feelings that keep you disappointed. It is an emotional addiction to disappointment. You derive pleasure from the low you feel. In an article in *Psychology Today*,[7] Nancy Colier says:

> When disappointment and hurt have been deep and consistent, there can develop a paradoxical pleasure in the experience of suffering. We feel a sense of validation and satisfaction in being let down again and again, a strange enjoyment and comfort in proving our negative experience to be true. We continue proving to ourselves and the world that we can't get what we need, and, underneath that belief, that we don't in fact deserve it. The ongoing disappointments confirm our rightness and establish a truth that can be relied upon, unlike the rest of life, and people. There then grows a masochistic pleasure in our own unworthiness, a satisfaction in being proven as undeserving. This distorted gratification then becomes a habitual substitute for getting what we really want, which is not actually disappointment.

When you continue to perpetuate the same set of feelings by not understanding why you do what you do, you end up holding on to events that you are in denial of or have repressed. These repressed feelings create your anxiety and depression. That's when the medical community wants to medicate you. When you medicate yourself because you are emotionally overwhelmed, you have no responsibility to change.

To break through, you must take responsibility for everything in your life—and not in your life. When you are responsible, you can respond. You are not reacting or overreacting. When you can respond in the present moment, you will no longer hold on to the past. This is how you step into power. In this power, your attractor factor changes. You attract to your reality people who are of like mind. You no longer attract people who want to get in the ring with you and put you into a position that you have to validate, justify, and explain. When you are no longer the mind-body connection to the events that shaped your feelings, you are in the process of becoming the person you deserve to be.

Ask Yourself

1. What area or situation in my life is causing me to live in force? What would I have to do or let go of to start living in power?
2. Where does codependency show up in my life? How did I become this way?
3. In what areas of my life is disorganization

getting in the way of my success? What mental clutter or chaos is creating it to manifest physically?

FOR COMPANION RESOURCES, GO TO
https://goldenmastermind.com/breakthrough-factor
PODCAST: Releasing Rescue Consciousness

FIVE

MASTERING YOUR EMOTIONAL STATE

Stuffing Your Feelings

Stuffing your feelings is a direct reflection of the events that shaped them. Many people find themselves stuffing their feelings with food, drugs, alcohol, compulsive spending, underachieving, under-earning, anorexia, bulimia, or any other multitude of addictions. Addictive behavior keeps you in fight-or-flight and overwhelmed.

Stuffing your feelings means you are repressing them. The most common way people stuff their feelings is with food. We are an overwhelmed, overweight society that stuffs our feelings with sugar, trans fats, genetically modified organisms, and other foods that taste good.

Many people carry excess weight on their bodies because they are chronic stuffers. This addiction can easily shape-shift from food to other addictions. But if food has been your drug of choice, start by uncovering where your chronic stuffing began.

If you're a food addict, there is a high probability that your addiction started with your mother or grandmother. Often food addicts secretly eat with one of their parents. They are told not to tell their other parent. They start to eat sweets together. They lick the bowl and pan together. They make cookies, sweets, and treats, and this soon becomes a way of life. Then, as an adult, food becomes the reward system when they finish a project, make it through a long week, or have a stressful day.

Many people also white-knuckle the feelings they stuff. They make it until the end of the night, and then they relapse right before they go to bed. They believe they deserve it because they have been good; they deserve a treat.

Food used as a reward system comes up in many families. It is used as a way to guilt the families together. Have you ever been guilted to fill your plate and finish it? This is one way people in your family use guilt to control you. If food has been a way to bond together as a family, it is time you understand how food becomes an addiction.

Children are often controlled by food as a reward system. A parent might say:

"If you are good, I will buy you an ice-cream cone."

"If you behave, you can have a cookie."

"If you get an A on your report card, I'll take you to the candy store."

Also, consider how the educational system has conditioned us around food. There are holiday parties with candy, cupcakes, and cookies. How many of your teachers gave you candy or food for getting an answer right or behaving properly? There are programs being used in schools to promote reading that offer a coupon for a free pizza from a major chain. These are the events that shaped your behaviors.

Then, as adults, many people stand in front of their cupboards or refrigerator and eat right out of them. I have also seen people eat right out of the aisles of a supermarket. They pick up a bag and start eating before they get to the checkout register.

Another commonality that leads to stuffed feelings is anxiety about controlling an outcome. This is the main component of why people experience avoidance. Controlling an outcome can lead to fear of flying, fear of driving across the bridge, or anxiety about driving on a freeway. I have coached many clients who have these anxieties.

I have pointed out on numerous occasions that the fatality rate of the airline industry is in one of the smallest percentages of all transportations. There are more automobile accidents where people lose their lives or are injured than ever occur when flying. If you fear flying, what you have is anxiety about an outcome that has not happened. If this is you and you are committed to letting go of the cause that creates the effect, look at why you do what you do.

Controlling the Outcome

Control is an illusion. You are not in control. When you are trying to control your control, you are out of control. When you let go of control, it liberates you. But if you have challenges seeing the other side of recovery, it is because you are in control of the emotional state that you continue to repress, stuff, and hold on to.

An addict always wants a little more. This is why so many people have challenges letting go of an addiction. The addiction is their identity. When you are emotionally addicted to a set of feelings, then you are in control of those feelings. Letting go of those feelings would change your identity. This will put you in a position where you would have to be responsible.

For you to be responsible, you have to be accountable. Most of society has challenges with changing their identity because they are responsible for being an addict. If this has been a way of life for you, then your ego will do everything in its power to keep you in a place called familiar. This is why so many people are stuck in avoidance.

If you are a chronic avoider, there's a high probability that you will fall behind in many areas of your life. You will fall behind on your taxes, your mortgage, your student loans, and many other situations. If this is you, then avoidance allows you to stay in control of these situations.

If you are reading this content and having an aha moment, that means you are starting to understand why you do you do. This is the point where you can decide to let go of control.

Let me be clear: there is no control. You are not going to be able to control what time the plane takes off or what happens once you get on the plane. When you let go, you gain command of your emotions. You start to be in a more relaxed body. That is when you are in the energy of joy, love, bliss, enlightenment, prosperity, and reciprocity. You step into flow rather than stay in resistance. You no longer fight with yourself, wrestle over how you are going to get something done, or worry about outcomes that have not happened.

Living in Worry

When you're a chronic worrier, then worry has become your identity. Where does worry come from? Worry has deep-seated roots in events from childhood experiences. If you had to take care of someone as you were growing up, there is a high probability that you continually worried about him or her. If you grew up with unpredictable, passive-aggressive people in your circle of influence, then you most likely worried about getting in trouble. As you are able to separate your feelings from the events that shaped them, you no longer repress your feelings. You no longer attempt to control an outcome.

I am not suggesting that you do not set goals and achieve them. That is different, however, than having anxiety about outcomes that have not yet happened. When you have clarity about the outcomes you are in the process of creating, that is consciousness. When you have anxiety about outcomes that haven't happened, that is control.

As you begin to let go of control, you will change your emotional state. You will be present. You will spend less time worrying about situations that have not happened. You will step into your power. You will release the mind-body connection to the events that have shaped your anxiety.

Here's an example of living in control. I once asked my local chiropractor if he would be open to meeting another top-tier chiropractor that I hired to give me concierge service. I was flying the concierge chiropractor to my home city to spend a day with my staff and me. I offered my local chiropractor the opportunity to be a part of the experience and mentor under my top-tier concierge service chiropractor for the day.

My local chiropractor immediately started to get anxious. He said, "Well, I'm not sure if I can learn like that. That seems really difficult. It feels like a lot of pressure. I feel like you put me on the spot." I explained to him that I wasn't putting him on the spot at all. I was simply offering him the opportunity to mentor with someone I was paying to receive top-tier service.

My local chiropractor eventually agreed to watch the procedures and also volunteered to let us use his office. However, the very night before the appointment, my local chiropractor came down with an ailment. He was not going to be able to attend the session the next day. He never gets sick, but it was so interesting how, at the very last minute, he became ill.

I know there's a high probability that he got

overwhelmed, telling himself a story about an outcome that had not happened. He was so in control of his control that he was not sure he could control the outcome. He created a story and the anxiety that he would not be able to perform up to my expectations. But I did not have any expectations. All I asked was if he would be willing to witness the event and perhaps learn from some of the techniques.

It is likely that he had created so much anxiety about an outcome he could not control that what he could control created an illness. Because of the illness, he would not have to embarrass himself by not being able to perform to a set of standards he believed I was expecting of him.

In reality, there were no standards. He had created a story and tried to control the outcome. He started to repress and stuff his feelings, which created his own dis-ease. This led to him becoming sick. This is a classic story, one I have seen many times. I have seen people get so overwhelmed about events that have not happened that they begin to magnetize to their reality the very situation they seek to avoid.

If you grow up with unpredictability in your household, this situation creates a mind-body connection. As a child, you would get overwhelmed by the thought or the probability of getting in trouble or being punished. You would be afraid of making a mistake, resulting in having to validate, justify, and answer to one of the perpetrators, violators, or passive-aggressive personalities in your circle of influence.

In childhood, if you get singled out, if you make mistakes, or if you get traumatized and picked on while at the playground, then your emotions are going to create a corresponding response. This is why you will end up stuffing your feelings while trying to control an outcome that has not happened.

A lifetime of overwhelming feelings that you have held on to has kept you in a low vibrational emotional state under-earning, underachieving, and not living your dreams. This relegates you to tiptoeing quietly through life, trading time for dollars in someone else's dream of a place called a job.

There is nothing wrong with having a job, but if you do not enjoy your job, it's likely you will have anxiety about that career. If you're seeking to change careers and committed to living the good life on your terms, it is your responsibility change your identity. It is your time to reinvent yourself in free enterprise or another career.

Many of my clients seek to be entrepreneurs but have been employees for a large percentage of their lives. It is common for an individual in this situation to go into fight-or-flight about the possibility of changing their identity. This can lead to anxiety about the outcome. The easiest way to neutralize that anxiety is to take a deep breath and realize that you are going to learn a new set of skills and habits, and you are going to improve your mindset.

When you start to let go of the anxiety, you can perform in a relaxed body. In this state of being, you can release and let go of the feelings that create scarcity and poverty consciousness. You can adapt and adjust easily and effortlessly. This skill is also required when it comes to neutralizing difficult people.

Neutralizing Difficult People

Occasionally people who are either in your life or enter your life will put you in a position where you have to validate, justify, and explain yourself. These are the types of people who use force and want you to be their counterforce. As you have a better understanding of this dynamic, you will learn to be and stay in your power.

Neutralizing angry and aggressive people is a skill. As you have a better understanding of human behavior and how predictable human beings are, you will start to have the advantage. You will be able to spot people who are putting you in a position of having to explain yourself.

It is not uncommon for people to ask me why I live in the city I live in. What they really mean is, "Why do you live in a cow town? A city that went bankrupt? A city in the heart of the United States mortgage collapse? Why do you live there?" This is a situation where people attempt to put me on the spot. I am very clear on the dynamics of what is transpiring.

I have also had people look at some of my accomplishments and attempt to diminish them. If you have people in your circle of influence that do this, it is likely they are passive-aggressive. These types of people find flaws in you and in the world. They want you to validate, justify, and explain yourself.

Early in life when you encounter situations that create anxiety, it is common to stuff your feelings. The anxiety comes from living in unpredictability. You are anxious about what might happen. Anxiety is created by growing up in a family with violence, addictions, anger, or a sibling that resented you and picked on you. You believe you are going continue to get traumatized, violated, and bullied. Your brain becomes emotionally addicted to a set of feelings. This creates a corresponding response based on a past event that triggers anxiety about a future event.

As you understand how childhood events continue to show up in your life, you can begin to neutralize them. You can let go and separate your feelings from the events. You can release the mind-body connection to the past. When you choose to do this, your life will begin to change. But you can also choose to be a maintenance addict tiptoeing quietly through life, barely getting by. If the pain is great enough and you are ready to let go of the events that shape these feelings, then it is imperative that you learn to neutralize difficult people.

If you are worried about offending the people who violate you, you will protect your perpetrators and violators. I see it all the time. This is what I hear: "Well, they're really not bad people," or "Well, they're my family . . . what am I supposed to do?" What you are supposed to do is have a better understanding of why you do what you do. You let go of the guilt about the people that violate you. You let go of the resentment that you stuff. You step into your power and no longer experience the mind-body connection to the events that overwhelm you. You no longer let people use guilt to control you. When you do that, you can neutralize people.

When someone says to you, "I can't believe you're not coming home for the holidays," you will learn to use their name and say, "John, what is it you don't believe about me coming home for the holidays?"

"We're going to miss you. It's family. I can't believe you're going to miss out on this."

You can reply, "I can appreciate your concern, but I'm going to have to pass this year." And if they persist, you are going to have to say, "John, what part of 'I'm not able to attend' are you not hearing from me?"

If you are thinking, "Oh wow, I could never do that," you're right. You've already taken yourself out of the equation.

If you have anxiety about offending someone, getting in trouble, or making mistakes, then you will continue to justify why you do what you do. As you start to let go and have a better understanding of people's predictability, you will develop the reflexes to neutralize conflict. If someone says to you, "I can't believe you quit your job," you will be able to say, "Susan, what can't you believe?" This is a technique where you take the person's name and package it in a question using the words they used to put you into position to justify yourself. This is called a U-turn.

Here is another example. If you ask me why I live

in Stockton, California, I'm going to ask you, "Do you have a city you suggest I should live in?" Often I get this response, "Well, well, well, I didn't mean to offend you." Now I can ask, "What did you mean?"

It's also crucial that you have the right tone when you communicate like this. You do not want to be aggressive when someone is aggressive with you. You neutralize aggression with peace. You take the edge off your voice and volley a question over the net to the other side of the court. This requires acute awareness. You cannot get overwhelmed, flustered, or tongue-tied. You have to be able to confront the issue by being objective, honest, open, and understanding of why people do what they do.

Someone who typically puts you in a position to explain yourself does this because they get a neurochemical high from the banter that goes on in this type of conflict. These people thrive on putting people in positions where justification and validation are required. Bullies, passive-aggressive and narcissistic personalities, and the flaw-finders of the world derive great pleasure by seeing you squirm. They like to watch you get overwhelmed.

As you begin to identify these people, you can uncover their agenda. Then you can live in your agenda—which is no agenda because you're not looking for conflict. You do not want to be right. You want to walk away from these conversations feeling good about yourself. This will be a breakthrough for you. You are no longer feeling rejected, abandoned, resentful, or guilty. You are living in a conscious, aware state from which you can adapt and adjust quickly.

Reacting versus Responding

Let's dive a little deeper into understanding why you react instead of respond. When your body goes into a fight-or-flight, that's a reaction. When you open your mouth and have to validate, justify, and explain yourself, that's a reaction too. When you don't know what to say, who to be, what to do, when you say *um* frequently, when you use the word *guess* frequently in your communications style because you don't know how to communicate, you are reacting.

You are reacting to past events that you hold on to consciously, unconsciously, and subconsciously not knowing why you do what you do because your whole childhood was a blur. You had great parents. You had great people in your circle of influence. In reality you are living in denial. You don't understand why you do what you do.

There are three main types of reactors: the ① aggressive reactor, the ② passive-aggressive reactor, and ③ the passive reactor. The aggressive reactors like to put people on the spot. The passive-aggressive reactors are full of contradictions. They love you one day and are in conflict with you the next day. The passive reactors are the ones who constantly are sensitive and defensive, feel picked on, and live in an overwhelmed, checked-out state—over-obligating, enabling, and doing more for others so they can deflect their low self-esteem.

Many people who react are addicted to controlling an outcome. This is why they avoid outcomes they can't control. A classic example of this is when people avoid success. They say they're avoiding failure, yet they fail to execute, which leaves them disappointed—the ultimate contradiction.

If you're committed to no longer living like this, you will begin to let go of living in an overwhelmed, unorganized state of consciousness. You will begin to have a better awareness of when your body is triggered into fight-or-flight. You will take a deep breath and release your past. You'll start responding to the stimulus differently. If you react instead, you'll react the way you've always reacted to stay emotionally addicted to a set of feelings.

As you start to respond, your communication style improves. You are able to neutralize passive-aggressive personalities. You don't feel put out, put upon, or put on the spot, and you're not under a lot of pressure. You don't create illnesses or disease; you never get sick. And if you come to one of my events and I ask you this question: "What do you do when you get overwhelmed?" you'll state in front of the audience, "Jeff, I don't get overwhelmed."

I live in this state myself. I seldom get overwhelmed. I have taught myself over a long career how to be in a state of alignment. I have clarity. I don't want to get even. I don't want to prove people wrong. I'm recovering from my hate, resentment, anger, guilt, shame, abandonment, and rejection.

Those are the primary emotions that drove my unconscious and subconscious and kept me emotionally addicted to a set of feelings that led to fourteen years of drug and alcohol abuse. I eventually hit rock bottom on three different occasions that led me to many indiscretions, discrepancies, pathological lies and a whole series of rock bottoms—THAT is "the pain is great enough" syndrome.

I was a chronic reactor. I was a victim being victimized by society. I had been victimized by certain people in my past and was holding on to that and holding them responsible for my feelings. As I learned to let go and step into my power, I started to neutralize some of those feelings about past events that no longer served me. I taught myself how to respond using a different set of reflexes.

Top-tier skilled athletes, firefighters, police officers, military professionals, paramedics, and others who operate very efficiently and effectively under adverse situations have the ten-thousand-hour habit under their belt, meaning the repetition and experience to be able to respond. However, most of society reacts because they find flaws, they get overwhelmed, they're negative, they're anxious, they live in guilt and shame, they've been rejected and violated, and so their body runs their brain. And this is why so many people stay in a relapsed, overwhelmed state.

It's common for me to hear people react by saying, "Oh, this is so big. I don't know where to start. I don't know. I don't understand my childhood. I had great parents. I had a great childhood." You had a great childhood, but you're hundreds of thousands of dollars of debt, overwhelmed, and overweight, holding on to a set of feelings that keep you emotionally addicted to anxiety.

Now, as you become honest—rigorously honest—and have a better understanding of why you do what you do, your body starts to align with your brain, and you become one. This is where you become more skilled at responding, and you're able to easily and effortlessly let go. You are no longer the mind-body connection to the events that keep you reacting.

Reacting is also connected to stuffing your feelings. It's controlling the outcome. When you've learned to neutralize difficult people, you respond to the stimulus differently, which means you're not reacting to the past. When you learn how to respond, now you can become responsible. You can live on a higher level of responsibility. You can become accountable. You can only account for what is familiar when you're a reactor.

When you are a reactor, you react to stimulus based on the events that shaped your feelings. As you commit to the process of letting go, the process of recovery, your body will respond differently to stimulus. You are virtually wiring a new brain. The neurons that wire and fire no longer have a shelf life. You no longer feel the way you felt. You no longer feel rejected when someone doesn't buy from you because you're learning how to respond.

The more you understand that human beings are

predictable and the more you're able to easily and effortlessly let go, the more you will be able to spot certain personality types that you will avoid. You're also able in conscious awareness to create connections on command with predictable people who are warm and friendly. And these are the type of people that are going to empower you in your life.

Becoming a Student of People

When you become a student of people, you'll understand the four different personality types:

1. the analytical thinker
2. the A-type personality
3. the life of the party
4. the amiable relator

I cover this in great detail in an eight-CD audio program called Personalities for Success: The Animal Factor now available as a digital download at goldenmastermind.com. It breaks down the four different personalities, their conditioned behaviors, predictability, and their likes and their dislikes. You also learn how to communicate with them, how to neutralize them, how to collaborate with them, and how to walk away from certain personality types.

When you become a student of the science of personalities, you understand predictability. This is going to come from changing your awareness, not being intimidated by people, not talking yourself out of the opportunity to connect with people, and committing to meeting people of influence and affluence. As you master your emotions, you can conduct relaxed conversations, qualifying people for your time, your energy, your products, your benefits, your features, and your romantic endeavors.

Whether it's in business or in life, you want to be able to look for the signs and the clues. When you ask someone a question, if they avert their eyes and answer with sounds and tell stories, this lets you know that this person has probably checked out. It means the person is overwhelmed emotionally, especially if they do it frequently. As you have a better understanding of why people do what they do and understand conditioned behavior, you can start to live in recovery.

Reconnecting to Your Breath

As children, we are naturally diaphragmatic breathers. As we experience pain, trauma, and go through events that violate us, our natural diaphragmatic breathing then transitions into high chest breathing. This keeps your body in fight or flight.

When you encounter an aggressive or passive-aggressive personality, it is likely that you will freeze up. You may lose your voice or become emotional. What happens is that your body remembers a past event and reverts to believing it is still in the past.

I had a client come to me for coaching for this very issue. Whenever she would get into a conflict situation, she would either freeze up or start to cry. She would get angry with herself because this would happen. She didn't understand why she wasn't able to say what she wanted to say. She said she could feel many emotions and then couldn't put words together to speak. She would feel embarrassed and shameful. I worked with her to uncover the events in her life that created this reaction.

Together, we uncovered that she had an angry, passive-aggressive parent. She never knew when she was going to get in trouble. This kept her in fight-or-flight and in a short breath syndrome. She wasn't able to connect to her power because all of her energy was being held in the upper part of her chest. She had also been through some violations for which she held herself responsible. She didn't speak up at the time of the violation for fear of getting the violator in trouble. This created a pattern of doubt about speaking up for herself.

As she was able to understand how the events in her life created her reactions, she began to become aware in the moment when her body would enter fight-or-flight. In the beginning, she still was unable to speak, but she knew what was happening. I remember her telling me when she really started to break through. An authority figure had asked her a question, and she froze. She couldn't think of how to answer. She realized that she was trying to find the answer she thought the authority figure wanted to hear. She was looking for the *right* answer. The authority figure finally dismissed her. She realized what had happened to her and took five minutes to reconnect to her breath. Her body calmed and she went back and was able to have the conversation.

Over time, my client was able to release the old patterning and stay grounded. Today, she no longer cries or freezes up. She has let go of shameful feelings and found acceptance. She committed to finding her voice. She broke through.

If you find yourself in a similar pattern of fight-or-flight, you too can break this pattern by reconnecting to your breath. Breathing can be used to train the body to release anxiety in stressful situations. Deep breathing stimulates the parasympathetic system—the rest and digestion part of your autonomic nervous system that calms you down.

When you are no longer the mind-body connection to the events that have shaped your feelings and identity, you can move into the flow of life. The goal of letting go is more than just getting rid of negative emotions and addictions. The ultimate goal is total freedom and total peace. Once you let go of resistance and you surrender, you can reprogram your neurological network one deep breath at a time.

Claiming Your Power

As you begin to step into your power, you are going to let go of your anxieties. Force requires an outside force to thrive, but power can stand alone. The power that I'm discussing is emotional power, not physical power.

Your objective is not to overpower. Your objective is to *empower.* You start first by empowering yourself, by loving yourself, by letting go, by understanding you are a soul having a human experience and you deserve your best.

As you focus on being your best one day at a time and stop putting pressure on yourself to be *the best*, you will begin to shift your emotional state. You will be in a more relaxed body. It's that type of power that raises your consciousness.

A new state of consciousness will change who and what you attract. This will change the emotions that you emanate. This will change the emotions that create a corresponding response. This is how you magnetize to your reality like-minded success seekers. This is the *science of attraction.*

As you start to claim and live in your power, you become powerful in a nonlinear equation. I'm not talking about physical prowess or power. I'm talking about emotional power, the attractor factor, and quantum leap-type energy where the sum becomes greater than the whole of its parts. When you begin to live in your power, you will be able to attract other people who are in their power.

As you focus on empowering other people, you will become a mentor, a leader; you'll be able to shape other people's beliefs and attract people who believe what you believe. You let go of control and begin to create powerful suggestions. You'll create ideas.

When you start to come from *why*, you start to have whys. A *why* is a clearly defined goal about an outcome you believe to be purposeful. That type of purpose magnetizes other purposeful souls looking for human experiences that can empower them.

When you are in this kind of power, you are the mind-body connection to the reality of the events you are creating on command. This is where you start to create synchronicity. A thought and a feeling together create a form. That form has a bounce-back effect to you.

As you live in this consciously aware state, you will begin to attract and command more frequently situations that empower you. If you continue living an overwhelmed, anxious, undisciplined, and unorganized state, you will frequently attract people to fulfill your feelings. You will avoid success to fulfill your disappointment. But as you understand why you do what you do and you are committed to letting go, you will step into your power.

Ask Yourself

1. What situations create anxiety that leads to me stuffing my feelings? What tendencies or addictions do I use to stuff my feelings?
2. In what ways do I attempt to control the outcome of a situation?
3. What are the main situations I worry about? How does worrying interfere with my ability to break through?
4. Who in my life (currently or in the past) is aggressive or passive-aggressive toward me?
5. What situations put me in a position to justify and explain myself?

FOR COMPANION RESOURCES, GO TO
https://goldenmastermind.com/breakthrough-factor
AUDIO: Mindfulness Meditation Audio

SIX

EMOTIONAL RELEASING

Letting Go

Letting go is one of my favorite topics to teach. It is often misunderstood. Letting go is not physical. It's nothing you are holding in your hand. Letting go is an emotional release. It's the ability to separate your feelings from the events that shaped them.

Holding on is living in control. Letting go is releasing control. Many people control their control until they are out of control. What do I mean by this? For example, take a person who lives in fear of leaving a relationship. He or she can't control what will happen when the relationship ends. What can be controlled is choosing what is familiar and predictable. The person attempts to control their emotional pain and life changes by staying in the relationship.

The challenge with holding on to a situation that does not serve your highest good is that it will keep you in low vibrational states of being. Your control allows you to feel safe but disappointed. You feel anger and resentment for being stuck where you don't want to be. Your level of control deceives you into believing you have no other options.

I hear this all the time: "Yeah, but . . . you don't understand. My situation is different." No, it is not. You are not special. The problem you have is not new. People have more challenging obstacles than you, and they overcome them because they let go of the emotional control.

A large percentage of society operates in overwhelm. They say, "I don't know. I don't understand. I'm not sure." This is a doubt state of consciousness. They hang on to anger, hate, resentment, guilt, shame, abandonment, rejection, grief, and apathy. The reason that many people hold on is that they can't see themselves letting go. When you are emotionally addicted, letting go would contradict your identity.

"Who would I be if I didn't worry? Who would I be if I wasn't overwhelmed?" You would be able to let go. "But how do I do that? How do I? How do I? How do I? I'm not certain. I'm not sure. I don't know why I do what I do." That's how the analytical, egoic mind gets addicted to a set of feelings. When you begin to have a better understanding of why you do what you do, then you can move into the "let go" phase of your life.

Let's take a look at the "How do I let go?" state. Instead of asking, "How do I let go?" ask yourself, "Why don't I let go?" This question allows you to uncover why you avoid change. When you can answer with rigorous honesty, you raise your awareness. You discover why you do what you do. You understand why you hold on—why you live in control.

To start the letting go process, take a deep breath.

The breath releases the neurons that wire and fire together based on familiar feelings. Breathing helps to reset your nervous system.

Many people live in a short breath syndrome. This keeps their body in fight-or-flight and disconnected from their power center, which is located in the pelvis area. Proper breathing assists you to stay connected. People that have been traumatized and abused often have outer body experiences. Staying connected to your breath helps keep you grounded and in your body.

Holding on is a survival tool. We think we are protecting ourselves by staying where life is predictable. Letting go feels unsafe. But by letting go, we release this programming. In his book *Letting Go: A Pathway to Surrender*, David R. Hawkins does an exceptional job of explaining the letting go mechanism:

> Letting go involves being aware of a feeling, letting it come up, staying with it. And letting it run its course without wanting to make it different or do anything about it. It means simply to let the feeling be there and to focus on letting out the energy behind it. The first step is to allow yourself to have the feeling without resisting it, venting it, fearing it, condemning it, or moralizing about it. It means to drop judgment and to see that it is just a feeling. The technique is to be with the feeling and surrender all efforts to modify it in any way. Let go of wanting to resist

the feeling. It is resistance that keeps the feeling going. When you give up resisting or trying to modify a feeling, it will shift to the next feeling and be accompanied by a lighter sensation. A feeling that is not resisted will disappear as the energy behind it dissipates.[8]

Letting go is a skill. You must develop it until it becomes a habit. You can't *try* to let go. When you try, tomorrow was really yesterday. You fail before you start. Letting go is a commitment to your breakthrough process that you practice daily.

"All I have to do is *just* let go?" Letting go is not "justing." It's not jousting. It's not wrestling. It's a state of consciousness where your pain no longer serves you. It's releasing the cycle of addiction. When you let go, you stop worrying about future events that haven't happened. As you change your emotional state, you change your brain. This process is what allows you to break through.

Breaking the Cycle

To let go of an emotional addiction, you must first understand the addiction cycle. The cycle begins with a stimulus followed by a corresponding response. Next you receive a pay off for engaging in the addictive behavior. Then the cycle begins again.

Addictions are a result of unresolved issues held in your body. An addicted brain will recreate the same situation repeatedly to fulfill a feeling. That's the cycle. When you break the cycle, you are no longer the mind-body connection to the events that led to your addictions.

Here is an example. You get into an argument with your boss who continually berates you. You want to quit, but you fear you won't be able to replace the income. You stuff your feelings of anger and resentment. When you see your boss the next day, you remember the argument and relive the event in your mind. The same feelings arise. You stuff them down and continue to work in a job that is not serving your emotional well-being. The fear of leaving what is familiar is too high, so you stay and suffer. To get rid of the negative feelings, you may resort to drinking wine every night, or you head to the vending machine for a chocolate bar to get a hit of serotonin and dopamine during your workday. This is how an emotional addiction shape-shifts into a physical addiction.

Physical addictions are rooted in emotional addictions. To break any addiction, you must address the cause that creates the effect. That is how you break the cycle. You get to the point where you decide. You commit. You say, "I'm so done with this!" You begin to set clearly defined short-term goals. Breaking the cycle means there are no more cheat days. Breaking the cycle is a breakthrough.

When you practice the repetition and experience of breaking through, it becomes a habit. Letting go becomes a habit. Relapsing is not an option. You create a new mind-body connection that frees you from the past.

Releasing Approval-Seeking Behavior

As a child, I went to great lengths to win awards. I would put in the time at the gym, the weight room, the track, and hitting the books at the library. I would do all this to be recognized for my accomplishments. I was reward- and recognition-conscious. My ego and self-confidence thrived on it.

If you haven't received the approval you were seeking, often you will develop approval-seeking behavior. This is what happens based on events of not being recognized, of being abandoned, neglected, forgotten, or rejected. This in turn affects your self-esteem—your ability to be comfortable with yourself. Your ego wants approval. Your higher self doesn't require it.

Recognition is not a bad thing. The challenge comes when you let recognition and being recognized become your identity. What happens when you don't get recognized? Do you tell yourself you are not good enough? Do you lose your identity?

Your goal is to approve of yourself. Respect from others will follow. When you disrespect yourself with self-criticism, you stay the mind-body connection to the unresolved events from your past. Your objective is to be recognized and rewarded for the person you are becoming. You don't have to have status to love yourself.

Releasing Co-Dependency Tendencies

In chapter four, I discussed the relationship between

guilt and codependence. I want to dive deeper into this subject because it is so prevalent. To gain emotional sobriety, you require releasing codependent tendencies.

Codependency breeds guilt and resentment. Many people stay in relationships that are unhealthy and even violent because of their guilt. They can't see themselves letting go. They don't want to leave someone behind. They are in control of what will happen to the person if they are not their caretaker. People move their perpetrators, violators, and their passive-aggressive family members into their home to fulfill their feelings of low self-esteem, guilt, resentment, abandonment, and rejection.

Consider the following questions:

- Did you lose your innocence in childhood?
- Did you have to be grown-up before your time?
- Did you have to give your money to your family to help support the household?
- Did you have to take on the role of a babysitter for your siblings?
- Did you have an alcoholic parent for whom you took on the role of caretaker?

If you answered yes to any of these questions, it is likely the cause of your conditioned behavior as an adult.

Codependency has its roots in enabling. To break the cycle of codependency, you must detach yourself from the people who have become dependent on you. If you operated as a caretaker in childhood, there's a high probability that you have become neurochemically addicted to a set of feelings that has you repeating the situation now.

Codependents often confuse the concept of serving versus being in service. If you have a database, clients, or teammates, you want to deliver exceptional service because you receive compensation for your value. Rather than give service, codependents are serving. Service is noble in certain situations. However, if serving is your identity, you are going to come last. You will do a lot of activity and actions but not get compensated for your value. When you aren't compensated for your value, it can lead to feelings of rejection. You may feel abandoned. Then resentment rears its head.

To break the cycle of codependence, you must understand the role you played as a child. It was either appointed to you, or you did it because you were reliable. To break through, you must commit to independence. You must set healthy boundaries. If someone attempts to use guilt to control you, you have to neutralize this person, so you don't over-obligate yourself. You have to be able to say, "I'm not going to be able to take on that role. I'll have to pass on that." When you can put yourself first, you break the cycle.

Releasing Victim Consciousness

An important part of the breakthrough process is to understand victim mentality. Blaming other people for your challenges gives your power away. You are then relegated to having your emotional state controlled by what someone else does or says.

Victims don't like to admit they are playing a victim role. Victims have low energy. They are sensitive and defensive. They find ways to be disappointed. They set people up to disappoint them. Victims are also flaw finders.

Being a victim is more comfortable than taking responsibility for your actions and reactions. If the problem is someone else's fault, the victim sees himself or herself as the *good one*. The other person is the *bad one*. Gossiping and complaining about the person who is the bad one gives the victim a boost of self-esteem.

Victims focus on the negative. They find the flaws in beauty. Victims go out of their way to create drama and chaos. They go outside of themselves to point the finger instead of focusing on what is going on internally. Only when a person begins to take responsibility for their role in the situation can they begin to overcome their challenges.

The truth is that many of us have been victimized. The goal is not to let being a victim become your identity. To do this, you must address the events when you were victimized. If you were violated, it is not your fault. But it is your responsibility to understand how being victimized created your emotional state. The event happened to you, but you are not the event.

Being a victim is often a direct reflection of being rejected, abandoned, neglected, or violated sexually, physically, or emotionally. If you grew up in a household where you had an older brother or sister who picked on you or if you went to school and were chronically bullied, this is the cause of where your victimhood began. This creates a corresponding emotional state of feeling rejected. When you've been victimized, being rejected becomes an emotional state that is frequent. It's a feeling that you create to fulfill the feelings of unresolved past events.

If you tell yourself, "I don't know why I do what I do," you will stay stuck. You hold on to feelings based on how you've been victimized. It's your responsibility to take the next step. To break through, you neutralize your feelings based on past events to stay consciously aware. When you take responsibility for your emotional state today, you move from being a victim to a victor.

Releasing Doubt

Doubt is the space between fear and faith. There is no leap of faith in recovery. There is just faith. When you begin to believe that you are lovable, that you are good enough, and you raise your level of expectations, you won't attract the same people and situations to fulfill being a victim. When you can let go of doubt, you no longer have one foot on the dock and one in the boat.

Doubt is the safe place where many people live because they don't have to make decisions. Doubt is a place where commitment-phobic people live. This is why they create statements like, "Yeah, uh-huh. I'll get around to that later. Yeah, why don't you get back with me." Doubt feels safe because you don't fail. The challenge with doubt is that it leads to disappointment because you don't succeed.

When I am coaching my clients, I hear statements like, "I don't understand why I do this." I reply, "What's your payoff?" And in response I hear, "Payoff? There is no payoff." Really? You wouldn't do what you do if you didn't get a payoff from it. The payoff you receive by being in doubt is that you don't have to perform. You don't have to commit. You don't have to be responsible, and you don't have to be accountable.

The more you understand why you live in doubt, the more you'll see that your comfort zone is often your failure zone. When you have anxiety about failing, you create your failure zone. Instead of putting energy into succeeding, you are giving in to anxiety about failing.

Taking Responsibility

Responsibility means "the ability to respond." Many people react to situations instead of respond to them. This is why they feel victimized. Your reactions are derived from your beliefs and expectations about an event or person. No one makes you feel a certain way. No one makes you cry. If someone speaks to you rudely and your reaction is to cry, the person did not make you cry. No one can make you feel a certain way. If you cry, that is *your* reaction.

To take responsibility for your feelings, you have to understand the cause of your tears. It's likely that your body is remembering a familiar feeling from the past. When you perceive an event in your present as an event from the past, your body is running your brain. You are in an addictive emotional loop.

To break through, you must uncover the cause that creates the effect of your reactions. This process is how you take responsibility for your emotional state. The game will change for you when you harness the power of decision. You decide to no longer be the mind-body connection to the events that shaped your emotional reactions.

Responsibility is your code of honor. This strength goes hand in hand with commitment and self-discipline. Responsibility means you claim your power to affect results and stop blaming your problems on external circumstances. Responsibility is the ticket to freedom that takes back your power from outside events and other people.

Taking responsibility for everything in your life—and for everything not in your life—means that you move out of denial. It means that you move into an acceptance state. You begin to accept who you are, and you are committed to being in a different emotional body. That kind of honesty and commitment will allow you to live in a balanced emotional state. When you start to understand that the magic is in you, you will begin to be the man or woman you are capable of becoming.

Ask Yourself

1. In what ways do I engage in codependent situations? What events shaped my codependent behaviors?

2. What situations or events from the past or present tend to bring up feelings of being a victim? How can I take responsibility for no longer being a victim?

3. In what area of my life does doubt show up most often? What creates my feelings of doubt?

4. In what areas of my life do I require taking more responsibility to create change?

FOR COMPANION RESOURCES, GO TO
https://goldenmastermind.com/breakthrough-factor
PODCAST: Releasing Resistance: Committing to the Process
VIDEO: How Do I Let Go?

SEVEN

RECONDITION YOUR SUBCONSCIOUS MIND

Changing Your Beliefs

To change your beliefs, you must first uncover what they are. If you are seeking a financial breakthrough, examine your beliefs about money. If you are attempting to find your soul mate, review your beliefs about relationships. In both scenarios, explore how you were conditioned growing up. What was communicated to you about these topics? Were there any significant events that shaped your current beliefs?

There are many subconscious programs running in your brain that override your conscious thoughts. You can say affirmations to change your beliefs, but it's likely that the subconscious programming will override them. Affirmations are important, but they have to be coupled with reprogramming your subconscious mind. Bruce Lipton, PhD, discusses the power the subconscious mind has over our beliefs in his book, *The Biology of Belief: Unleashing the Power of Consciousness, Matter & Miracles.*[9]

When it comes to sheer neurological processing abilities, the subconscious mind is more than a million times more powerful than the conscious mind. If the desires of the conscious mind conflict with the programs in the subconscious mind, which "mind" do you think will win out? You can repeat the positive affirmation in that you are loveable over and over or that your cancer tumor will shrink. But if, as a child, you repeatedly heard that you were worthless and sickly, those messages programmed in your subconscious mind will undermine your best conscious efforts to change your life.

It may seem like a daunting task to change your beliefs, but don't fret. If you are committed to your breakthrough process, it can be done by using hypnotherapy, visualization techniques, meditation, EFT tapping, Neuro Linguistic Programming, energy psychology modalities, and understanding the cause that creates the effect.

Start by uncovering the emotions attached to your beliefs. Explore how the emotions are connected to your past. Here are a few examples.

"Geez! Why did I do that?" In this statement, the underlying belief is that I am not smart. The emotions attached to this belief are guilt and shame.

"My husband is such an idiot." The emotions attached to this belief are anger, resentment, disappointment, and victimhood.

"I'm not good enough to be loved by her." The emotions attached to this belief are unworthiness and shame.

Once you have uncovered the emotions attached to your beliefs, begin to separate your feelings from the event that occurred. When feelings of shame arise because you lock your keys in the car, recognize the feeling. Take a deep breath and release judgment. You get to choose what meaning the event receives. Is it something to feel shameful about, or is it a simple error in judgment? Begin to affirm a new belief.

Let's take this a step further. Your beliefs will determine your action or inaction. Your beliefs are your sense of certainty or your sense of uncertainty. When you are certain, you will trust your feelings. If you are uncertain, you will rely on reasoning, facts, figures, data, and research to make a decision. You will spend a lot of time processing, being overwhelmed, and avoiding decisions.

The language of belief and certainty use superlatives like *yes, unequivocally,* and *absolutely.* When you are uncertain, you will speak with an uncertain communication style. You will say, *Uh huh, yeah, okay, yep,* and *sure.*

The most common word that telegraphs your

uncertainty is the word *guess*. Many people insert the word guess mid-sentence without knowing it. On coaching calls, I've encountered clients that say *guess* over twenty times in a fifty-five-minute coaching session. "I'm going to stop eating at fast food restaurants I guess, and then that should help me to start losing weight." In this example, you can see the person is unconsciously telegraphing their doubt.

When you are uncertain, you are telegraphing you are overwhelmed and can't make a decision. When you can't make a decision, you will avoid. Procrastination can be a result of low self-esteem. You don't believe in yourself, so you avoid doing a task or achieving your goals. Your behavior is a direct reflection of your beliefs.

I recently spoke to a young woman who told me she was having challenges landing the job she desired. Even though she was highly qualified, she was unable to land these jobs because of her disbelief. She was going into her interviews subconsciously saying, "Please hire me, but don't because I'm not good enough. I'd really like this job, but I'm uncertain. I'd really like to join your team, but I'm not sure I wouldn't sabotage myself, so I'm going to blow the interview."

In her mind, she didn't get the job before she even walked into the interview. When you have conflicting beliefs, feelings, and thoughts, you are sending an energetic mixed message. The people you interact with sense it. You cannot achieve your goals if your beliefs are limiting you.

The best time to change your beliefs is now. Many people choose not to change their beliefs because it would contradict their struggle. It would be the end of the era—the death of their ego. To change your beliefs, release the emotions attached to them. As you create new beliefs, you are changing your identity. Your beliefs guide your life. Through awareness you can release the beliefs that do not serve you.

Deserving and Receiving

The word *deserve* comes from the Latin term *deservire*. It means "day of service." When you become comfortable and skilled at receiving, you will no longer live in the mixed message. If you don't feel good enough to receive, often the cause is based on past events of violation, transgressions, abandonment, rejection, or trauma. When you are in a mixed message, what you are saying is, "I'm not certain that I deserve this."

Because I speak all over the United States more than forty-five times per year, I encounter many service-oriented people. I believe in rewarding exceptional service with gratuities and tips. I watch many of these people check out, get overwhelmed, and make statements such as, "I can't accept that. I'm not sure if I receive that. What is this for?"

I've offered twenty dollar tips to busboys, maitre d's, people that work in service-oriented situations, and they become overwhelmed and uncertain if they should receive the money. They look around and wonder if they are going to get in trouble. The reason people react this way is they are not comfortable receiving based on the events that shaped their lives. As you begin to let go and separate your feelings from the events that shaped them, you won't question your deservability.

Have you heard the phrase, "It's better to give than receive?" Think about this for a moment. Why isn't it equally as important to receive, as it is to give? In reality, it is. There should be a balance in the two situations. You should be skilled at giving and receiving.

Many people are unable to receive a compliment. A compliment contradicts their beliefs about themselves, so they deflect it. Sometimes they don't even hear it. In more extreme cases, people will put you in a position where you have to validate and justify your compliment. Here's an example. "Susan, you've really improved over the last year." Then she replies, "Really, I don't think I have. Why do you say that?" And I reply, "Why do I have to justify my compliment?" If you are uncomfortable receiving a compliment, start by saying *thank you*. Over time it will get easier as you continue to work on your receiving skills.

Your Dialogue with Money

Your dialogue with money is going to be a direct reflection of the twenty thousand meals you spent with the people you grew up with. Your dialogue with money will also determine your ability to ask, receive, and deserve. It is also dependent on your ability or inability to create transactions in free enterprise.

There are connotations about receiving, deserving, and money that hinder people. Having money doesn't make you a good person. Having money doesn't make you a bad person. Money responds to people who are comfortable with the creation of it. A skilled drug dealer can create money just like a skilled business owner can create money. Money is not the root of all evil. Money is a requirement for you to purchase goods, products, and services. Catherine Ponder teaches in her book *The Dynamic Laws of Prosperity* about the origins of the myth that being in poverty is spiritual.

The feudal systems during the Middle Ages assured wealth only for the privileged few. During this period, the teachings of "poverty and penance" were offered to the masses as the only way to salvation, in order to keep people in poverty, and to make lack and privation a supposed "Christian virtue." Unsuspecting millions were led to believe that it was "pious to be poor," a belief which was useful in forestalling revolution among the masses. Some of those old feudal ideas about poverty as a spiritual virtue have persisted until today, but they are false, man-made ideas and not God's rich Truth for you and me.[10]

To change your dialogue with money, you must uncover the mixed messages you have been taught about money. Many people don't know why they have challenges receiving and deserving. Often it is lack of self-esteem based on past events. You can be confident and competent and still have no self-esteem. You can be confident at a job, but the same person who has low self-esteem and a high self-confidence will have challenges starting a business because he or she doesn't feel good enough. The person will get overwhelmed. The person won't know what to do, how to act, or know what to say. He or she will overwhelm themselves in the details. This keeps the person approaching and avoiding business ownership.

If you don't feel comfortable with yourself, you will be in a mixed message. You will deflect opportunities that come your way. You will end up sabotaging and alienating the people you seek to attract.

A job will pay you what a job is worth. If the job isn't worth much, then you won't be paid much. People let their feelings about their job determine their self-worth. If you are underpaid, you may be resentful for not being compensated adequately. In a job, you don't get paid what the free market will bear. If you want to create value in free enterprise, then it's imperative you feel comfortable creating the kind of commerce and transactions that will allow you to live a good life.

The value and service you bring to free enterprise will establish what the free market will bear for you. If you want to be a millionaire by owning your own business, you are going to require customers, clients, transactions, and money moving in and out of your bank account. You are going to require the skills, habits, and mindset of a millionaire to accomplish this goal. Your inner dialogue determines your ability to receive, deserve, and ask. To be able to create more money, your dialogue with the outcome must shift.

Releasing Self-Sabotage

Sabotage plays a significant role in the belief that you don't deserve to have it all. It interferes with your long goals. Sabotage can be subtle or flagrant. People with emotional addictions commonly end up sabotaging themselves. Self-sabotaging behavior results from a misguided attempt to rescue yourself from negative feelings. Here are a few of the most common sabotage patterns. Each is followed by a description of how they limit your belief systems.

Resignation

Deep down I don't believe I deserve it, so I won't even go after it. I don't like to get my hopes up, because then if I don't achieve my objective, it won't hurt so much.

Throwing It Away

I get it, and then because I don't believe I'm good enough, I throw it away. This sabotage is widespread in professional sports, especially with athletes from terrible home lives.

Settling

I think I want it, but I'm not sure I'm good enough, so I'll settle for less. I won't try very hard, because I probably won't get it anyway.

Denial

I won't pay any attention to this problem. Hopefully, it will just go away.

The Fatal Flaw

People who use this strategy may advance themselves by taking all the right steps, but they have a crucial personality problem—perfectionism, excessive drinking, being a hothead, an overreactor, or have overwhelming guilt that undoes all their best efforts.

Blaming

This is probably the most common of all the sabotages. Everyone, everything, and every excuse are used to place blame except on the right person. This is a way to intellectualize all the reasons not to take responsibility for both actions and lack of actions.

Poor, Poor, Pitiful Me

This sabotage is very common with people who are ill or injured all the time. These people have a chronic problem usually related to getting attention.

Poverty Consciousness

This stems from the programming of grandparents and parents. It is the by-product of lack and scarcity. It's thinking that money is tight or there is never enough.

It's assuming you will lose it if you have it. Poverty consciousness involves the mentality of "holding on to whatever you have or you will lose it."

When you have sabotaging self-talk, you will energetically project mixed messages. These mixed messages can be both verbal and nonverbal. They wreak havoc on your own self-perception, and they can have negative consequences for your relationships, whether business or personal.

"Please don't buy from me so I can feel abandoned, rejected and disappointed."

"Let's just hang up the phone now so I can prove myself right. See, this always happens to me."

What each of these sabotages has in common is an underlying sense of not deserving the desired goal. The key to changing your subconscious sabotages is to become explicitly aware of your *internal deserve quotient*. Your deserve quotient is comprised of your conscious and unconscious beliefs about what you can and should achieve in life. Once you uncover these beliefs, you have the power to change them.

As you release self-sabotaging behaviors, you let go of being your own worst enemy. You stop listening to the critical self-talk in your mind. Self-talk—the way you communicate with yourself—determines the way you communicate with others. Consider how you communicate with yourself.

- Do you judge yourself?
- Are you able to receive a compliment?
- Do you feel unworthy?
- Do you get frustrated with yourself?
- Do you deserve success?

Your self-talk must be conducive to an emotional state that results in healthy self-esteem. The books you read, the audios you listen to, and the people you surround yourself with influence the way you think and the way you talk to yourself. Begin to study successful, prosperous, healthy individuals. Listen to the way they speak. Watch the actions they take. As you learn to upgrade your self-talk, new patterns will emerge in your life. Your self-talk is the fundamental key for either breaking through or staying where you are.

Ask Yourself

1. What limiting beliefs do I require changing to break through?
2. In what situations do I have challenges deserving or receiving? What are the events that shaped my beliefs about deserving and receiving?
3. What are my beliefs about creating and receiving money?
4. Do I have any sabotage patterns preventing me from breaking through? If yes, what pattern or patterns do I require releasing?

FOR COMPANION RESOURCES, GO TO
https://goldenmastermind.com/breakthrough-factor
BLOG: The 10 Worst Decisions You've Made With
Money: Connect and Disconnect the Dots Exercise
VIDEO: Your Dialogue with Money: The Terms
Surrounding Money

CHAPTER EIGHT
MAKING YOUR VISION A REALITY

Creating Your Vision

Do you remember when you were ten years old? What were your dreams? What about at age fourteen or twenty-one? What did you want for your future? Now, answer this: What are your dreams now? When I ask people this question, I hear about paying off credit cards and mortgages. I ask, "Is that what you dreamt about when you were fourteen and twenty-one?" Today, it's time to dream again.

When you start dreaming, you can create a vision that's worth pursuing. Your vision is your guide. It's your compass to take you to the good life. If you don't know where you are going, how are you going to get there? Vision is the ability to believe in the magnificence of your dreams. It's the outcome you seek.

Many people's vision of the future is anxiety. They worry. They wonder. They get overwhelmed about what hasn't happened. And they magnetize and attract to their reality the very situation they seek to avoid. They say, "I hope this doesn't happen to me." Unfortunately, they communicate a mixed message, and their vision is a vision of overwhelm.

You want to create a vision you can romance. Your vision should motivate you to spring out of bed each morning to take action. Start simple. Ask yourself the following questions:

- What kind of people do I want in my life?
- What does my ideal day look like?
- What type of romantic partner do I want in my life?
- What does my health look like?
- What kind of a physique do I desire?
- What experiences do I want to have?
- What does my family look like?
- What type of income am I seeking to create?
- Is there philanthropic work I would like to do?
- Where do I want to live?
- What type of home do I want?

These questions should assist you to focus on the outcome you seek. A vision is not something you write on a piece of paper and never revisit. Your vision is your daily inspiration. To be intentional each day, many people create vision boards and put sticky notes on their bathroom mirror. Meditation, prayer, and visualization are all great tools to assist you to make your vision a reality.

Many people have big goals, big dreams, and big aspirations. The challenge is they have ten-cent habits. Creating a vision alone is not enough. You must develop an action plan and execute it daily. This means you have short-term goals and long-term goals. You have a ninety-day action plan. You are responsible and accountable to your vision and your goals. When your habits, mindset, and skills are in alignment with your vision, your breakthrough is inevitable. As you create your vision, you can find your purpose.

Purpose-Driven

I was an addict for fourteen years. I was destitute during the last couple of years in my addicted state. I lost the will to live. I lost my vision. I had no purpose.

When I got clean and sober at age thirty-one, I felt renewed. I felt like a new lease of life had been given me. It was a second chance. I committed to myself that I would never relapse again. I have been able to master my emotions to accomplish that task. No relapses. No reverting to my old self. I am here, now, and present one day at a time. My purpose is to live a good life. In my speaking, coaching, and writing, my purpose is to teach people how to break through so they can live a good life as well.

To be purpose-driven is to find a niche that inspires you. You may not know your purpose right now, but it's vital that you find it. "I want to be a millionaire." That's a great goal, but for what purpose? What happens when you reach financial success? Have you then lost your purpose?

I am living my purpose. I found my calling. I've been doing exactly what I've wanted to do for over twenty years. Through this content, my objective is to assist you to find your purpose. Living a good life should be one of your purposes. You determine what a good life means.

Become a Goal Getter

Goals are what you create to monitor your progress. They are meant to motivate you to take action. Goals are what inspire you to achieve. They give you a sense of accomplishment. Goal getting is when you go for the gold medal, the championship ring, or the trophy.

Goal setting is a science. You don't want to set goals so big that you won't be able to achieve them. Recently I asked a client what her financial goals were for the upcoming year. She replied, "I want to be a millionaire." This was a bold goal considering she was only making four hundred dollars a month in her network-marketing business. If you want to be a millionaire, you have to have a millionaire's skills, habits, and mindset. I assisted her to see what type of income she would have to produce per day, week, and month if she wanted to achieve that goal. By the end of the coaching call, she created a practical goal. Becoming a millionaire is still part of her vision. But to be able to achieve that goal, it has to be laid out in an achievable manner.

You require short- and long-term goals. I recommend that you set goals for your day, your week, your month, ninety days, six months, a year, and two years. If you own a business, how many prospecting and follow-up calls will you make today? How many sales will you close this week? How much income will you create this month? These are the type of questions you ask yourself when you are goal setting.

Your goals are your plan for success. They must be clearly defined. For example, you may have a goal to pay off your debt. To add clarity to that goal, add a date. The goal would be, "I will be free of debt by December 31st of this year." Then ask yourself if it is an achievable goal. Once you set your goal, create a plan to accomplish it. How much will you pay off per month? What will you do to create the money to pay it off?

Your goals must also have meaning. Choosing an arbitrary monetary number as income goal can lose its luster after achieved. Ask yourself clarifying questions:

- Why do I want to achieve this goal?
- What will achieving this goal give me?
- Why do I want what it will give me?
- Why do I want to achieve a $250,000-a-year income?
- What do I want to do with the money?
- Do I want to take a trip?
- Where do I want to go?
- Why do I want to go there?
- Who do I want to take with me?
- What type of accommodations am I seeking?
- What experiences do I want to have on my trip?

These are a few examples to gain clarity and paint the picture of the why behind your goal achievement.

Many people set goals but never take the appropriate

action. Some people never start, or when they do, their effort doesn't last long. They're not sure they can accomplish the goal. Look at all the people who make New Year's resolutions to lose weight. They create a goal but don't commit to it.

Goal achievement requires engagement. You cannot achieve a goal by sitting on a bench. You cannot reach a goal by wishing it will happen. Daily emotional discipline is what leads to goal achieving. Goal setting and goal getting are why you play the game of life. Goals give you a sense of certainty. They give you a sense of gratification.

Goal setting is an ongoing process. You may not reach all of your goals in the time frame you set. You also may blow some of your goals out of the water. There is no end game. There is always another level to achieve. As you continue to set and achieve your goals, you are breaking through.

Accountability

There are times you may have a hangnail, a headache, the flu, feel overwhelmed, or anxious. Being accountable means you will suit up and show up. You will deliver. The show must go on. What does that mean? It means that you must be accountable. A producer, a closer, and a finisher all find ways to overcome challenges and obstacles.

When you are accountable, you do everything in your power to meet your obligations. That doesn't mean you don't take a day off if you are sick. But when you are accountable, you do what is required to meet your responsibilities.

Many of my clients have part-time businesses. Their goal is to become full-time business owners and quit their job. What tends to happen is that people can be accountable in a job because there is a set of rules to follow. But there are a different set of skills, parameters, and blueprints you must operate within when you own a business. You have to be accountable to yourself. You are the boss. You have to be your best employee.

Owning a business means that you must be accountable for your time. You don't get paid an hourly wage. You get paid for production, service, and value. Your responsibility is to turn time into results.

Accountability is being honest with yourself. You may have heard the phrase, "The fortune is in the follow-up." That may be true, but you require being able to follow up and follow through with your commitments. Finishing must become an identity.

Many people have a procrastination identity. They have bad habits and avoid taking action. Their challenges are a reflection of the stories they tell themselves.

"If I avoid accountability, then I don't fail."

"If I avoid success, I don't fail."

The truth is you fail because you don't engage. Success is based on an engagement principle. You must be able to engage your prospects. You must also be able to engage your fears and anxieties. That means you confront others and confront yourself in a relaxed body.

Many people start and don't finish. They are chronic avoiders. If you want to succeed, you have to pay the price. You have to be a master of discipline. That means you master your emotional state, you learn the skills, and you develop a daily method of operation.

A committed finisher is someone who focuses on the outcome. To be a finisher, you have to become clear about what you are capable of accomplishing. No matter where you have been or what you have been through, you can unequivocally change.

Change is a choice. It's a commitment and a decision. It is a one-day-at-a-time process. When you focus on the emotional discipline one day at a time, you will stay in the game long enough to master the skills of your vocation. Lack of emotional discipline is what leads to avoidance and procrastination. When you can chunk your vision and goals down to one day at a time, the story about it being hard or difficult diminishes. The goal is to develop the emotional discipline that assists you to complete tasks and produce results.

Success is not difficult to master. Your emotions are the challenge. If you don't master your emotions, then you are trying to control your emotions. Control is force. You cannot force yourself to be in peace. Control overwhelms you.

Overwhelm is about the stories you tell yourself. You get so worked up that you can't produce results.

You don't take action. You don't finish what you started. Overwhelm is why people get ready to get ready. When you get ready to get ready, you create dust. You don't blaze the trail. For you to blaze the trail of success, you have to enter the unknown.

When you focus on results and solutions, then the problem doesn't seem so big. The stories you tell yourself create doubt. Uncertainty drives you to opt out instead of staying the course. When you let go of doubt, success becomes a certainty.

Accountability is completion. It means you are completion-conscious. You finish what you start. When you are accountable, you find a way to overcome a challenge rather than focus on the problem. When you focus on the problem, it creates anxiety. When you focus on a result, your body releases. The body is no longer overwhelmed in frantic energy. To be accountable, you must let go of the noise in your mind that says, "How am I going to do this?" "How am I going to pull this off? "I'm not smart enough." "This is too hard." Accountability is when you can stand the gaff, and you don't listen to the voices that say, "I can't."

I have a long-time friend and client that use to live in Austin, Texas. He was a top income earner in a small start-up network marketing company. He went through some challenges and realized that he wasn't cut out to have a job or own a traditional business. He packed up his belongings and moved to Nashville, Tennessee.

He committed to pursuing his love of music. He is a singer, songwriter, and guitarist. He plays in honky-tonks, juke joints, and bars. When times were tough, you could find him playing for money with his guitar case open on the street.

He's been playing music now for over twenty years. He is accountable for his goals and his dreams. This past year he has performed over three hundred times. If he doesn't make it to the big leagues, I guarantee he will still be in Nashville playing the game. He will not live the pain of regret. He will not die with his music inside of him. He's motivated because he is inspired to live his dream.

Becoming Self-Motivated

To many people, their goals and dreams may seem like a mountain. When you are self-motivated, you don't require someone else to motivate you to make the climb. You are going to scale that rock until you reach the peak.

Most of us have been groomed, raised, and conditioned to have a job or go to college so we can get a job. We are used to someone else telling us what to do. We tend to operate from the "forty, forty, forty club." That is a forty-hour workweek, for forty thousand dollars, for forty years. Unfortunately, it typically only brings you a forty-dollar Timex watch.

When you have spent much of your life waiting for someone else to tell you what to do, it can be challenging to operate as an entrepreneur. You become the boss, and now you must tell yourself what to do. Most people who have a small business from their home operate their enterprise as though they were a nonprofit organization. They don't know how to motivate themselves to create profit.

Being self-motivated requires a different level of emotional energy. When you attempt to force yourself to do something, it is not likely to happen. You should not have to make yourself take action toward your dreams. Ask yourself these questions:

"Why do I get out of bed in the morning?"

"What dream will motivate me to spring into action when I wake?"

When you can see, feel, and believe in your dreams, you will be self-motivated. Simon Sinek perfectly explains the concept of knowing your *why* in his book *Start with Why: How Great Leaders Inspire Everyone to Take Action.*

It all starts with clarity. You have to know WHY you do WHAT you do. If people don't buy WHAT you do, they buy WHY you do it, so it follows that if you don't know WHY you do WHAT you do, how will anyone else?[11]

If you aren't buying into to your dreams, then your *why* isn't powerful enough. When you know your *why*, what you do has more meaning. Your *why* is a success tool. It is what drives you to break through. As you develop this clarity, your life is motivated by purpose. You live in integrity with your dreams because you are self-motivated by your *why*.

Your Sense of Urgency

Your sense of urgency determines your timeline for achieving a task or goal. It means you are relentless about reaching your goal. You are inspired to take action daily. You don't wait around for the right time because the right time is now. You decide first and learn as you go. There is no waiting until you listen to enough podcasts, go to all the trainings, and read a plethora of books. Having urgency means you are committed to taking action now.

Your sense of urgency should be a relaxed energy, not a frantic emergency. You cannot transform or change in an overwhelmed state. You don't perform your best when your back is against the wall. You perform your best when you are at ease. Relaxing means letting go and releasing the anxieties about outcomes that have or haven't happened.

Early in my recovery, I felt that I was behind the eight ball and behind in my life goals. I wanted to hurry the process. I thought I could make up in numbers what I lacked in skills. The challenge was, I was so intense that I was blocking my success. In 1990, when this was pointed out to me, it made me angry. I felt resentful, rejected, and hurt. I felt abandoned, and I began to pout.

The person who pointed this out to me let me know

that I was so intense that I was alienating him as well. I was alienating the very people I sought to collaborate and connect with because of my insecurity.

I had a sense of urgency, and I was trying to make up for lost time. As I began to relax, let go, and release, I started to speed up by slowing down. I was trying to speed up by speeding up—going one hundred miles per hour. As I eased off the accelerator and took my foot off the brake, I became more consistent in my speed.

I started to drive the freeway of life between seventy-five and eighty-five miles per hour rather than a one hundred to 120 miles per hour. As I began to live in relaxed intensity, I started to create a different sense of urgency. Rather than coming from a desperate state, I started producing from a relaxed state. Instead of being in a state of "I have to have it" state, I came from a state of "I'll create it as I go." I knew the results were going to come. I didn't know where they would come from, but I stopped being attached to when they would arrive. As I began to live in detachment, I started to create a different result.

Then I had a magical year. As I experienced the law of alignment, practically everyone I was seeking in the past six years showed up in a one-year period. It was the breakthrough year I had been seeking. I had changed my emotional state. I had changed who and what I attracted. I put emotional and physical discipline into to mastering my sales, branding, and marketing skills. I became proficient at changing my beliefs, my ability to receive, and my deserve level. I started to develop a new dialogue with myself:

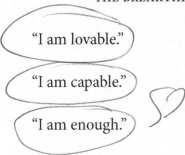

"I am lovable."

"I am capable."

"I am enough."

Throughout my life, especially my first thirty-five years, I was skilled at attracting money and equally skilled at losing it. Sometimes I would enable someone with the money I created so I could be in the same situation—financially challenged. Throughout my breakthrough process, I changed my dialogue with money. As I had a better understanding of what being a goal achiever was, I developed a sense of relaxed urgency. I became purpose-driven.

You, reading this content now, have the unequivocal ability to break through. Start with your vision, your goals, and a sense of relaxed urgency. Start with an inner knowing that you can achieve the outcome you seek.

Ask Yourself

1. What does the vision of my ideal life look like?
2. What are my short-term and long-term goals?
3. What does my ninety-day game plan look like?
4. What does having a sense of relaxed urgency look like and what I will do daily to achieve my goals?

FOR COMPANION RESOURCES, GO TO
https://goldenmastermind.com/breakthrough-factor
VIDEO TRAINING: Clarity, Focus, Concentration,
and Vision

CHAPTER NINE
THE HEALING PROCESS

Healing the Addicted Soul

Addiction is when your body runs your brain. When you hold on to the past, you will create subconscious and unconscious anxieties about the events that have shaped your feelings. When you memorize these states of being, your thoughts and feelings will become one. You are constantly reliving the past through how you think and feel.

Because addiction affects both the mind and body, many of us have to hit rock bottom to change. In my case, one rock bottom wasn't enough. My addictions led to many transgressions. In 1982 I hit three parked cars while intoxicated and then was arrested. In 1987 I was incarcerated for an incident that bought me nine months in jail. That didn't stop me from drinking when I was released. From there, I lived on my parent's couch in Iowa for a time until I returned to California.

My final rock bottom came when I was driving down the freeway and thought I was having a heart attack. In reality I was experiencing delirium tremors. My body was shutting down from my alcohol addiction. My drinking had gotten so bad that I had been consuming a gallon of vodka a day for two years. I ended up in the county detox in Stockton, California. Let me tell you, it was no Passages Malibu. This rock bottom was life or death. It was at that point my soul had suffered enough.

In the breakthrough process, you don't have to hit rock bottom. You can change at "rock now." You can take the first step in the recovery process by making a choice to no longer live the way you've been living. As you step into recovery and step into your power, you begin the process of healing.

The healing process never ends. When you are committed to the process, it becomes easier. You let go more quickly. You no longer hold on to the events that shaped your feelings. Your awareness heightens, and you can raise your level of consciousness by understanding the cause that creates the effect of why you do what you do.

As you let go of your anxiety, fear, and doubt, you move into a state of awareness called consciousness. That state of consciousness is where your body begins to heal. Your body can't heal when you are in fight-or-flight. It can't heal in an overwhelmed state either. Address your anxieties and the events that shaped them. That is how you address the cause that creates the effect.

When you understand the mind-body connections that have shaped your feelings, you will start to live free of dis-ease. That means you won't get sick as often. You won't get hay fever. The aches and pains go away because you no longer require the feedback from your body.

As you begin to heal your addicted soul, relapsing is not an option. There are no cheat days because the pleasure is not worth the pain. One drink is too many, and a thousand is never enough.

In the healing process, you step into the man or woman you are capable of being. You start to find your power and let go of force. You no longer hold on to what does not serve your highest good. Recovery is not hard. It is an experience you embrace.

Releasing Anger

Anger is an emotion that emerges from events. Your perception of an event is what creates your emotional state. Many people live with unresolved anger. They stuff the feelings from when something upsetting happened to them.

Some situations that create unresolved issues include:

- growing up in an unpredictable environment
- being raised by a passive-aggressive parent, grandparent, or caregiver
- experiencing a passive-aggressive sibling, neighbor, or individual in your circle of influence
- being bullied or picked on at the playground by your classmates
- being teased or made fun of by your playmates when you attempted to articulate your feelings

The way you perceive an event creates your feelings, your moods, and your identity. Events from your past are what created the anger that currently challenges you. You may have been violated, abused, neglected or abandoned. You may not have been able to please people in your circle of influence. You may have grown up with passive-aggressive, angry personalities in your circle of influence. The more you understand the cause that creates the effect, the better the opportunity and the awareness for you to let go of the events that shaped your feelings. But when a past event is stored in your psyche, there is a high probability that an outlet will be required to neutralize the feelings you continue to stuff. This is how angry outbursts emerge.

Many people are unaware of the correlation between fear and anger. Being angry is one way to mask fear from others and from yourself. Anger is a protection mechanism. It can be a way to shield yourself from feeling weak, ashamed, embarrassed, or vulnerable. Here are some ways it can manifest:

- Fear of rejection
- Fear of money
- Fear of success
- Fear of intimacy
- Fear of commitment
- Fear of responsibility

It takes a lot of emotional energy to stay in the struggle. It also takes a vast amount of emotional energy to stay broke, yet people who harbor anger continue to insist on struggling. When they are just about to turn a corner and reach the success they have been dreaming of, something happens that sabotages them.

Remember when you were a child, full of dreams and aspirations? You were free back then. You were naturally spontaneous. Where is that little child? What happened to those dreams? Keep asking yourself why, and eventually you'll get to the heart of the matter. Who stole those dreams from you? Who replaced them with anger, disappointment, and fear? Who conditioned you not to be successful?

If you're like most of us, by the time you were eighteen years old, you most likely heard the word no 144,000 times. Consider what type of philosophy about success your parents had. Did they encourage you to live life on your own terms or did you watch them struggle? All of this early conditioning formed your beliefs. Struggle, fear, worry, anger, and failure are part of the cycle of sabotage.

Anger can also attract conflict. When conflict is a way of life, you will attract people and situations to fulfill your feelings of being violated, traumatized, rejected, and abandoned. If you are angry all the time, live in disappointment, and create dramatic scenes to prove you are right, you have a conflict consciousness. Anger and conflict do not serve you. Anger alienates the people you seek to attract.

Here are a few questions I want you to ponder:

- Why do you often find yourself stuck reliving the past, not able to live fully in the present?

- Why can't you let go?
- What keeps you angry?

When I ask my coaching clients these questions, often I hear the answer, "I don't know."

To break through, you must move out of denial and get honest with yourself. Telling yourself you don't know why you do what you do only perpetuates the situation. Rigorous honesty is what will set you free.

To let go of anger, it is important that you learn to forgive and not hold other people responsible for your feelings. Your past events do not have to equal your present feelings. When you separate your feelings from events that no longer serve you, you no longer have the mind-body connection to the events that shaped your identity.

Anger was the main emotion that perpetuated my addictions. It kept me from breaking through for many years. I have a deep understanding of anger and resentment, which led me to write my previous book *The Anger Factor: Letting Go of Unresolved Anger*. If you struggle with anger, I highly recommend you read it to begin the process of letting go.

The Power of Forgiveness

Forgiveness is a powerful exercise that facilitates the healing process. By forgiving, you are not forgetting. You are not repressing. You are releasing. You objectively look at why you do what you do. You take responsibility for your mistakes and understand that they are simple errors in judgment. As you begin to forgive yourself for transgressions and events that led to your addictions, you will be less critical of yourself.

Being self-critical leads to feelings of guilt and shame. Your goal is to move into feelings of acceptance, willingness, and courage. As you progress up the scale, you move into love, joy, peace, and enlightenment. When you can go one whole day without being self-critical, that is a day of recovery. The state of noncritical behavior is where you begin to love yourself.

As you begin to forgive yourself, you are no longer the mind-body connection to the traumas and events from the past. When you start to live in rigorous honesty and practice forgiveness coupled with gratitude, your energy will change. Your breakthrough begins to take place.

Forgiving others is another critical component to healing the addicted soul. Forgiveness doesn't take someone else off the hook. It takes you off the hook. You are not saying what a person did to you is acceptable. Yes, the event happened to you, but you are no longer the event. It doesn't define you.

In forgiveness, you are not holding the perpetrator responsible for your feelings. When you hold someone else responsible for your feelings, you live in resentment. Resentment is a deep level of abiding anger. It is disease energy, the kind of energy that will create dis-eases in the body. It eats away at the heart. It eats away the soul. It can disrupt your immune system and your adrenal system.

To heal, you must learn to let go. Letting go means you can forgive. Forgiveness demagnetizes the subconscious and unconscious events that have shaped your feelings. As you practice forgiveness, you take off the yoke. You are no longer the mind-body connection to the traumas and events from your past.

Overcoming Adversity

Many of us have been traumatized and victimized in the past. We have been through many adverse situations. As you bring forgiveness into your life, you release the adverse situations you have held on to.

Adversity is not something you can avoid. You are going to win some, and you are going to lose some. It is part of life. Adversity is what pushes us to grow. In the breakthrough process, the way you respond to adversity must shift.

When adversity knocks on your door, how do you respond? Do you go into panic mode? Does it stop you from being productive? Do you feel victimized? Do you head to the refrigerator for comfort? Do you do you overreact? These are the questions to ask so you become conscious of your thoughts and behaviors.

One of the biggest obstacles to overcome is the story you create. Your story will define you as either the victim or the victor. The words you choose shape your story. "Oh . . . this is such a tragedy. I can't believe this is happening. What am I going to do now?" What you are going to do is assess if the situation is a tragedy or a challenge. Is it a tragedy or is it an inconvenience? Is it a tragedy or is it an annoyance? You have the power to choose. I will tell you this: you won't find the answer by drowning in the problem. You won't find the answer by swimming in a sea of sorrow.

If you find yourself encountering similar adverse people or situations, evaluate why you are attracting them. Ask yourself:

- What is the familiar feeling or emotion I am encountering?
- What disempowering belief does this situation reinforce?
- What requires healing within me?

It is vital that you understand how you become a vibrational match to adverse situations. If you believe there is never enough money, you send the message to the universe to prove you are right. Then, *bam!* The roof leaks. Your kids require money for their school pictures, and you get a flat tire. You have been rewarded with the exact situation to fulfill your feelings. To break through, you must change what you attract. Colin Tipping shines a light on this perfectly in his book *Radical Forgiveness*:

> Situations that appear to be the worst that could possibly befall us may hold the key to our healing something deep within us that keeps us from being happy and prevents our growth. The people who seem to us to be the most troublesome and the least likable may, therefore, be our greatest teachers. What we think they do to us, they do for us.[12]

To overcome adversity, you must first accept the situation. Pay attention to the story you create about what is happening or what you are predicting is going to happen. Monitor your emotional state. Bring it into balance so you can focus on finding a solution. Accept responsibility for the role you play in the situation. As you become solution-conscious, you will neutralize adversity quickly. Living in this state of mind attracts adversity less often. When you can address adversity in a relaxed body and an aware state of mind, you are breaking through.

Ask Yourself

1. In what situations does my body run my brain?
2. What transgressions or past events do I require granting myself forgiveness?
3. From whom have I been withholding forgiveness?
4. What adverse situation do I frequently encounter? What beliefs and emotions would I have to release to no longer attract this situation

FOR COMPANION RESOURCES, GO TO
https://goldenmastermind.com/breakthrough-factor
PODCAST: Understanding the Faces of Anger:
Identifying Anger Personalities

CHAPTER TEN
EMOTIONAL RESILIENCE

Committing to the Process

In one form or another, we are all overcoming emotional addictions. To break through, you must commit to recovery. To commit means to carry out or bind to a course of action. Recovery is a state of being. It's not simply quitting a behavior. Recovery is creating a new life. When you commit to the process of recovery, it means you don't come out of the process. You learn the inner game of recovery.

If you are committed to recovery, you are going to stay in recovery while you figure it out. You let go of being in your head. You release being overwhelmed in your analytical mind. You commit to understanding the cause that creates the effect. You commit to understanding why you do what you do. There is no end to the process. It's not a state of being recovered. Your recovery consistently evolves.

In recovery, there are no more cheat days. You transform. You excel. You become your best. In this process, you consciously grow. When you are committed to living a good life, you live it.

On the other hand, if you are a chronic relapser,

you will find ways to avoid success. Many people fear failure, yet they fail because they fail to execute. When you are committed to the process, you will execute. You will integrate and implement the necessary skills, habits, and mindset. You let go of being a human doing, and instead you learn to be a human being; you start to relax in your body. You let go of the repressed feelings that you stuff based on the events that shape your anxiety.

When you are committed to the process, you will become voracious at learning the skills required to be and stay in the process. The process is where the payoff is. The process is where you learn the inner game of why you do what you do. You are able to easily and effortlessly separate your feelings from the events that shaped them. Your awareness is heightened. You start to raise your level of consciousness. This is the breakthrough factor.

When you are committed to the process, you will not be denied. You will step into accountability and practice responsibility. You have to be responsible before you can ever be accountable. But many people avoid being accountable because they avoid being responsible. Even though the words *accountable* and *responsible* sound similar, these two words are distinctly different.

Responsibility is the ability to respond to the stimulus that is in front of you. Responsibility is different than a reaction. When you are responding, you are in command of your emotions. When you are reacting, you are overwhelmed by your emotions.

As you become responsible, you are able to

become accountable. When you are accountable, you are committed. Without commitment, there's no accountability. When you wing it, you have no system, no method, no routine, no resolve, no reason to stay in the game long enough to master the process. The process, accountability, paying the price, and tenacity all come together when you're committed.

Commit is a word that is seldom used in the English language. So much of society uses *need to, like to, guess, kinda, sorta,* and *don't know.* These are words of noncommitment. Read the following statements.

I'd like to break through.
I'm committed to breaking through.

I guess I should quit smoking.
I'm committed to quitting smoking now.

I'd like to eat healthier.
I'm committed to eating healthier.

Could you feel the difference? You might *kinda sorta* like to accomplish a goal, but it's never going to happen without a commitment. When you commit, you become accountable to yourself.

Accountability starts with making your bed. It starts with an exercise routine. It starts with planning your day and executing your plan. When you are accountable, you have a clearly defined vision of the outcome you seek—and you create it. This requires mastering your emotional state so you stay in the process. Accountability becomes a skill, a habit, and a mindset.

Building Emotional Resilience

Emotional resilience means that you move out of anxiety and into awareness. In emotional resiliency, you live in a state of recovery where you do not relapse. Many people relapse emotionally. This means they revert back to a familiar feeling. It's a neurochemical addiction.

To be emotionally resilient, you separate your feelings from the events of your past. This skill requires awareness and presence. Accountability to your emotional sobriety occurs when you interrupt a feeling in the moment and are able to neutralize it. You no longer allow your body to live in past events. Your body no longer runs your brain. Dr. Joe Dispenza explains how emotional addiction takes place in his book *Breaking the Habit of Being Yourself: How to Lose Your Mind and Create a New One*. He has spoken at several of my events over the years. His content is some of the best I have ever read about understanding the addicted brain.

> The brain constantly monitors the way the body is feeling. Based on chemical feedback it receives, it will generate more thoughts that produce chemicals corresponding to the way the body is feeling, so that we first begin to feel the way we think and then to think the way we feel.[13]

Emotional resilience means you are able to adapt and adjust to challenges that come your way without reverting back to a past event or becoming emotionally overwhelmed. You stay grounded and are solution-oriented.

When I was a freshman in high school, I was traumatized by three boys in a hazing experience. They held me down in the locker room and did some inhumane things to me. The boys told me that if I told anyone, they would do it again. As a result, I repressed the event and stuffed my feelings. This is one of several events that created feelings of violation, anger, and abandonment. I became the mind-body connection to the event. The repressed emotions are what let to my physical addictions. I let my body run my brain.

Later in life I was able to understand what happened to me, but I didn't have to let that event own me. It was something that happened, but I was not the event. Today, when a situation happens and similar feelings from the past arise, I am able to quickly let them go. I have emotional awareness. This is how I am able to no longer be the mind-body connection to the event. My tolerance for navigating adversity continues to increase.

The emotional tolerance most people live in is overwhelm. If you live in an overwhelmed, unorganized state of mind and body, you will have challenges mastering the moving parts of success. Emotional resiliency means mastering your emotions. You don't let your emotions take you out of the game. You don't shut down because you have a challenging moment.

You don't lie in bed all day because you are hiding from life.

When you are resilient, you focus on results. You don't let conflict or a roadblock derail you emotionally. You focus on solutions. You keep your eye on your goals. You may have moments that are challenging, but you don't linger in negative emotions. This means you don't have a bad day—only a few challenging moments.

You look adversity in the face, and you don't back down. You learn to be accountable to yourself, and you are willing to pay the price to break through. You gain the tenacity to overcome whatever comes your way.

Paying the Price

On this journey, the price you pay will be the full price. You don't achieve your goals by wanting and wishing. A select few might get lucky, but typically luck doesn't last. Personally, I'd rather be good than lucky. If you want to reach your goals and create success for yourself, the price must be paid. That means you do the inner work. You develop yourself. You learn new skills. You develop new habits. You continually evolve your mindset.

Your mindset should say, "Failure is not an option." This is why it's important not to compare yourself to someone else. When you see someone who is successful, you are seeing the glory. You don't know that person's story. You have no idea the price he or she has paid.

When you see someone else succeeding and you feel less than, let go of your anxiety. The only person you are competing with is yourself. Focus on going through the process. Complete simple disciplines one day at a time. Master repetition and experience to become successful.

Paying the price means you are tenacious about breaking through. Tenacity requires having a clearly defined vision of the outcome you seek. It requires short-term goals and a ninety-day game plan to accomplish them. It requires a daily method of operation.

Tenacity is fueled by your vision and measurable goals. To pay the price means you don't make excuses. You take action daily to reach your desired outcome no matter how you feel. You master your emotional state when the going gets tough. You let go of looking for a shortcut, and you pay the price.

Ask Yourself

1. What does being committed to recovery mean to me?
2. What will I do to become accountable to my breakthrough process?
3. What does paying the price require of me?

FOR COMPANION RESOURCES, GO TO
https://goldenmastermind.com/breakthrough-factor
VIDEO: How to Be Consistent as an Entrepreneur
BLOG: An Inside Look at How Millionaires Use
Time Differently

CHAPTER ELEVEN
AWAKENING TO HIGHER LEVELS OF CONSCIOUSNESS

Raising Your Awareness

Transformation is the art of change. Once you have a better understanding of what to change and how to change, you can practice the art of change. You will become a change agent. When you are in the transformation process, you change how you feel. You change how you look. You change the way you operate. You change how you've been changing. You are able to adapt and adjust as you raise your level of awareness.

When you are aware, you are no longer in a low level of emotional energy called *anxiety*. In awareness, you let go of causes that create the effect of why you do what you do. You are no longer in a state called *denial*.

In awareness, your energy changes. Your vision changes. You are able to see 240 to 360 degrees around you. Your sense of touch, feel, and hearing changes. You are able to hear what is meant, not merely said. Your intuition and extrasensory perception changes. You are able to connect to the quantum field, the energetic field of infinite possibilities.

People begin to notice your awareness. When you are aware, you are in a relaxed body. You are living in the present moment. You are able to see what's going on to the left and right of you. You are not in a place of trying to be perfect. You are in an effective energy, being able to adapt and adjust to the stimulus and situations that are going on around you. Your eyesight and your mindset shift. You live in a place called *know*—a place called *knowing*.

When you *know*, there is no doubt. Separating your feelings from the events that create your anxiety, your fear, and your doubt is how you raise your level of awareness. Your awareness is what changes your energy. As you become consciously aware, you will seldom attract the perpetrators, violators, over-obligators, people-pleasers, and overwhelmed people. You will be able to neutralize yourself emotionally by staying aware. When you are in denial and experience anxiety, you will attract to your reality people to fulfill your feelings— people who believe what you believe.

As you change your beliefs and come from a place called *know*, you no longer say, "I don't know" or "I don't know why I do this." You won't talk in riddles about how hard and how difficult something is going to be. In your emotional state, you change your corresponding response. You attract to your reality people and situations that foster your highest calling, your greatest good, and your purposes.

Changing Your Vibration

Your vibrational state is the emotional state that is communicated to and felt by others. All people emit vibrations. Have you ever walked into a room and felt the tension? Have you felt the energy change when someone walks in the room? What you are sensing is the vibrational frequency of the people around you. You can feel their emotional energy.

Your vibrational state dictates who and what you attract to your reality. When you live with low levels of energy, you attract people and situations to fulfill that level of vibration. If you are angry and resentful, you will attract people who cut you off in traffic. You will attract people who wrong you. You will attract conflict.

On the other hand, if you live in the vibrational energy of courage, willingness, acceptance, love, joy, and peace— you will attract people and situations to fulfill these positive levels of vibration. Ideal parking spots appear, a producer joins your business, or you meet your soul mate. Peace, prosperity, and ease become what you attract.

To break through, your vibration requires changing. The way you change your vibration is by gaining an understanding of why you do what you do. I have said this many times throughout this book because understanding your behavior is the foundational skill to the breakthrough process. When you understand why you do what you do, then you can make different choices. Your consciousness increases, which raises your vibration. This happens because you change the way you feel about yourself.

When you are able to let go of being critical, recovery begins. When you are able to master your emotions for one day, that's a breakthrough. Soon you will start to string days together, and then weeks.

We are so conditioned to either be positive or negative. What I'm covering for you here in this content is the middle ground called *objectivity.* As you are objective in a place called metacognition, you are able to think about how you've been thinking. You are able to evaluate how you've been evaluating. You are able to let go easily and effortlessly. You are able to be in a place called present moment awareness.

In that place, your energy begins to shift. Your emotional vibration begins to change. You let go of anger, hate, resentment, guilt, shame, abandonment, rejection, overwhelmed feelings, grief, and apathy. You are in your highest level of awareness. You are raising your consciousness. Your consciousness is your awareness, your state of *know*—meaning "I know."

When you know, you are in trust. You trust your feelings. You trust your thoughts. You trust your universe. You trust your God. You trust infinite intelligence. You trust mankind. You are able to adapt and adjust to trust. You don't operate from blind trust. You trust what you know. You trust your feelings. You trust your awareness. You trust your intuition. You trust your inner knowing. This greatly increases your attractor factor.

To raise your vibration, you learn to let go of the past, separate your feelings from the events that have shaped them, and release your attachment to the identity connected to low levels of vibration. You let go of the perpetrators, violators, passive-aggressive personalities, the people who have traumatized and hurt you. You no longer live in past events. You are no longer a victim. Yes, you experienced those events, but events are no longer your identity. As you form a new identity with increasing vibrational energy, you move into prosperity consciousness.

Prosperity Consciousness

Prosperity consciousness comes from the word *prosperity.* Prosperity itself comes from the Latin term *prospero*—meaning "in the flow." When you are in a prosperity state of consciousness, you frequently attract what you desire. When you are in a poverty consciousness, you attract what you do not desire. This fulfills your disappointment.

When you let go of your poverty consciousness, your broke thoughts, and your lack mentality, you begin to live in a higher level of awareness. You begin by developing the following skills:

- You feel deserving.
- You are open to receive.
- You release angry giver tendencies.
- You let go of giving for approval and recognition.
- You become productive at creating results.

When you become results- and production-oriented, you are moving into prosperity consciousness.

When you are prosperous, life begins to flow. You can let money go easily and effortlessly without concern that there is lack, scarcity, or not enough. When you change your dialogue with money, receiving, and love, you begin to attract prosperity more frequently.

On a flight you get upgraded to first class. Miraculously, someone next to you is a person of influence or affluence, and voila—they are open to having a conversation with you. You find yourself easily communicating, not worried about getting rejected or abandoned. You don't have an agenda. You're not trying to control the outcome.

In this type of prosperity mindset, you will attract frequently the hands-free zone. The hands-free zone is where you have your wrist on the steering wheel. You are able to take the curve with no anxiety about going off the cliff because there is no cliff. You are on the road. You are on the road to recovery. You are on the road to freedom. You are on the road to prosperity . . . *prospero . . . in the flow.*

In this hands-free state, in this enlightened body, when you become one with the universe, there is no separation between you and the result. That's the power of vision and the power of thought.

When you can clearly see the outcome you seek to create, you have already created it before you get there. You no longer attempt to *try.* "I'm not sure if I can see myself doing this." You won. You're correct. You spoke into reality the very existence you sought to avoid to fulfill your feelings.

It's better to be good and skilled than lucky. When you rely on luck, you are relying on a small percentage of the law of averages. When you live in enlightenment, synchronicity happens frequently—there are no accidents. Meaningful coincidences begin to line up. You decide to call someone you know and before you even pick the phone up, your phone rings and it's that very person that you were going to call. There are no accidents. You live in the law of alignment.

As you live in a vibration conducive to the good life, you are no longer in force. This becomes attractive. People feel it, sense it, see it, and want to be around it. This is where they say, "I don't know what it is about you, but I want to be part of what you are doing." In that state of enlightenment, you are able to be the person you once doubted you could be.

Prosperity consciousness means that you live in the law of plenty. You can't speak and think of lack and expect to attract abundance. To change your mindset, begin to change your expectations. Expect positive outcomes. Expect to succeed. Become aware of the thoughts and beliefs that keep you from accepting prosperity. What you think about affects your vibration and what you attract. To break through, change your consciousness toward money, success, acceptance, deserving, and receiving. Practice gratitude daily. Begin to align your thoughts, feelings, and actions with abundance. As you move into alignment, you will unify with prosperity.

The vacuum law of prosperity can be invoked in

this process. I have done this myself and watched many of my clients do it as well in their breakthrough journey. Catherine Ponder, who was a Unity minster, details the process in her book *The Dynamic Laws of Prosperity*.

> You have heard it said that Nature abhors a vacuum. It is particularly true in the realm of prosperity. The vacuum law of prosperity is one of the most powerful, though it takes bold, daring faith to set it into operation, as well as a sense of adventure and expectation to reap its full benefits. When a person is honestly trying to be prosperous, is thinking along prosperous lines and still fails, it is usually because he needs to invoke the vacuum law of prosperity.
>
> The vacuum law of prosperity is this: if you want greater good, greater prosperity in your life, start forming a vacuum to receive it! In other words, get rid of what you don't want to make room for what you do want. If there are clothes in the closet or furniture in your home or office that no longer seem right for you; if there are people among your acquaintances and friends that no longer seem congenial—begin moving the tangibles and intangibles out of your life, in the faith that you can have what you really want and desire. Often it is difficult to know what you do want until you get rid of what you do not want.[14]

When you let go of what no longer serves you, the space is opened for something new to take its place. If your life is cluttered with chaos, there is no room for prosperity. When you let go of anger, you make room for courage, acceptance, and love. When you release people that violate you, space opens up for people who support you. When you stop hoarding objects you might need someday, you open yourself to the financial means to purchase what you require. Living in lack and hoarding things you think you might need someday is not prosperous thinking. When you focus on what you might lose, you are in an energetic state of fear. Fear cannot attract prosperity.

The vacuum law of prosperity will be part of your continual breakthrough process. It is not a law that is only invoked once. Whenever you get to a sticking point, review what in your life you require to let go of. This can be a person, place, thing, idea, belief, or past event. Think of it this way: Let go of the lesser to make room for the better.

Ask Yourself

1. What situations do I tend to attract that are familiar?
2. What state of mind do I have to let go of to raise my vibration?
3. What thoughts are keeping me from creating a prosperity mindset?

FOR COMPANION RESOURCES, GO TO
https://goldenmastermind.com/breakthrough-factor
PODCAST: Principles for Prosperity: How to
Expedite Your Journey to Success
PODCAST: The Vacuum Law of Prosperity:
Making Room to Receive

CHAPTER TWELVE
TRANSFORMATION

Innovation and Creativity

Innovation is defined as the introduction of a new idea or a method. *Creativity* is the ability to create. When you combine innovation with creativity as a skill set, your level of consciousness will shift. These are the skills you require to address challenges and barriers.

Many of my clients own a business or seek me out when they no longer want to trade time for dollars in someone else's dream called employment. If your goal is to be self-employed, it is important that you understand what that means. When you own a business, you are in free enterprise. You can create and magnetize what the free market will bear.

In the free market, there are no limitations. What will separate you from the person you are capable of being is your innovation and creativity. Without these two qualities, you'll ask questions like:

"How do I?"

"Where do I?"

"I don't understand."

"Can you tell me?"

"Can you show me?"

"I'm lost."

"Oh my God. I don't know what to do."

"I'm out of business because I have no leads."

You're out of business because you have no innovation, no creativity.

When you have no innovation or creativity, you can't adapt and adjust. You are relying on the analytical egoic brain—the brain of reason. This is the brain that says, "Someone tell me what to do." When you have grown up in the educational system and have adapted to the left-right world, you are going to rely on reason and facts.

But when you live in your right brain and are innovative and creative, you will figure out how to overcome challenges. You are resourceful. This means you are able to activate the resources around you. Someone who goes from surviving to thriving will thrive in the jungle because of innovation and creativity. It's amazing how that person will find a way to find food. They create shelter. They find a way out of the jungle because of their ability to be resourceful.

When you become resourceful, you are no longer looking for the solution outside of yourself. You don't require asking a friend what to do. You don't have to ask the mailman if you should quit your job. You don't have to ask the dogcatcher for his opinion on your relationship. You don't look for someone to blame. You don't seek advice from someone in the same financial situation as yourself about whether you should start a business.

The person you ask is *self*—meaning *you*. When you seek answers outside of self, you are avoiding the problem. When challenges arise, this is an opportunity for you to grow. It's an opportunity for you to be innovative and creative. It's an opportunity to let go of anxieties based on the past and create a new neural network in your brain that says, "I can do this." When this process becomes a habit and a mindset, you can increase your level of performance.

Performing at Your Highest Level

Max Planck, German quantum theorist and Nobel Prize winner, said, "When you change the way you look at things, the things you look at change." This mindset is perfect to adopt in the breakthrough process. To break through, you can't live in doubt, victimhood, or any low vibrational state of mind that keeps you from performing at your highest level.

If you live in doubt, you are in the space between fear and faith. You have one foot on faith and the other on fear—not knowing where to go. You are not born with doubt. Doubt is learned based on how you were conditioned growing up. As you let go of the past, you will turn down the volume on the voice of doubt and turn up the voice of love.

When you come from love, acceptance, and personal responsibility, you no longer play the role of the victim. You are ready to be the victor. You are creating a new identity. In this new identity you come from your highest level of good; you come from your power.

When you are in power, you will perform at your highest level of energy. When you let go of the outcome before it happens and live in a place called the *law of detachment*, then you are not concerned about an outcome that hasn't happened yet. You will create your own outcome through your innovation and your creativity, performing at your highest level.

Moving into the Zone

Your highest level is called *the zone*. The zone is where you are able to create on command. Imagine on a whiteboard the number sentence "two plus two equal sixteen." Sixteen is greater than two plus two; the sum is greater than the whole of its parts. This is called the compounded effect, the 80/20 rule—where 80 percent is produced by 20 percent of your effort. When you break down the LOF—the law of the few—then you will be one of the few who breaks through.

Most of society is conditioned to tiptoe quietly through life and arrive at their grave safely. It's the toxic agenda. A large percentage of society will die of diseases brought on by their emotional state. They will be led to believe that it's cancer and other dis-eases, not understanding that the mind-body connection is what creates many of their challenges.

But you are different. You are here and you are now. You are breaking through because you are committed, and you no longer are going to live in a low emotional vibrational state. You are going to move into the zone—a place called *enlightenment.* In the zone, you can make a sixty-five-foot basketball shot like I did as a junior in high school: NBN—nothing but net. Now, that feat could not be duplicated. It only happens to one in a million. But because you are you and you are breaking through, you can create that one-in-a-million shot on command.

Recently one of my clients sent me a message saying:

> It's uncanny. It's miraculous. But of course, you taught me, and you teach all of your students. I pulled up to an event and the parking lot was absolutely packed. There was no one to valet park my car. I decided to find my own parking space. Before I could even go a few feet, someone right in front was backing out so I could drive right in.

That is the zone.

As a young boy, I used to practice riding my bicycle with no hands. In my twenties, I used to live in West Los Angeles. I would ride my bicycle in the morning from Westwood, California, down Santa Vicente Boulevard to Ocean Boulevard. I would walk my bike across the

Pacific Coast Highway to Will Rogers Beach. That destination was exactly 6.6 miles from my apartment. I used to ride hands-free in "the bike zone" three-fourths of the way there. I would put my hands on the handlebars only to stop at some traffic lights. I practiced until I mastered that skill.

That's the art of repetition and experience. It's the hands-free zone. The more you live in the zone, the more you will attract to your reality your highest good from an elevated level of consciousness.

Ask Yourself

1. Where am I wasting my time physically, emotionally, and/or spiritually?
2. In what situations does doubt hold me back from breaking through? What story would I have to let go of to release doubt?
3. In what ways do I play the victim in my life? How can I take responsibility for progressing forward right now?

FOR COMPANION RESOURCES, GO TO
https://goldenmastermind.com/breakthrough-factor
PODCAST: In the Zone: Transcending Levels
of Consciousness

THIRTEEN
BREAKING THROUGH TO SUCCESS

Living an Inspired Life

Inspiration is an attitude about how you approach life. It is not a "How do I?" situation. You are inspired because you are inspired. You know where you are going. You love life, and you love yourself. You set goals, and you are committed to them. You decide first and do what is required to accomplish the details later. When you are inspired, you are present. You are here. You are living in the now. You are willing to go through the process. You adapt and adjust to challenges and adverse situations.

People say to me, "What motivates you?" I tell them, "I'm inspired." This is confusing to most of them. They don't understand because they are not inspired. They are trying to be positive rather than inspired. When you "try" to be positive, you are going to fail before you start because you are not committed.

Everything I do is a task well done. I pick up trash on the road. I live a clean life. I do a lot of situations because it gives me joy. I do everything I can to the best of my ability. I'm no longer disappointed trying to be the best. I'm focused on being *my* best. It's in that flow that my life has meaning.

Being the best is overrated; there is always going to be someone better. When you are *your best*, you can accomplish that daily because you are living in a high level of awareness. This is how you raise your vibration. When you live an inspired life, you will attract other like-minded, inspired souls to collaborate with, cooperate with, be soul mates with, and become best friends with. You don't have bad days. You only have a few challenging moments.

Perseverance

Perseverance means doing something despite the difficulty or delay in achieving success. It's having tenacity, determination, and staying power. It means you don't listen to the voices in your head telling you to give up. You preserve because you see the outcome and you know in your heart and soul you can achieve it. You know it's possible. You don't let challenges, conflicts, or roadblocks take you out of the game. You adapt and adjust. You stay focused on a solution. Why? Because you know you can achieve it.

You have trust in yourself and your abilities. You have belief. You are willing to learn the skills and practice them daily. You develop the habits required to reach your goals. You look procrastination in the face and say, "No thank you. You've got the wrong person."

You surround yourself with people that encourage you and release those that don't. You are mindful of your thoughts, feelings, and beliefs. You are not willing to allow negative thoughts into your mind. You know they affect your mindset and focus. You feed your brain with new information through books, podcasts, and audio programs to reinforce your vision and purpose. You don't accept excuses.

Perseverance is a mental state. It may involve your physical body, but it's your ability to overcome the mind that propels you forward. Without persistence, you become a victim of your circumstances. Your energy drops and you move into a depressed state of being. You feel as though situations are happening to you. But what if your challenges are happening *for you*? They are your opportunity to grow. They are your opportunity understand more about yourself. What if adversity is your greatest teacher? If you didn't have challenges and hard times, how would you appreciate the times when you are in flow? Losing a game allows you to appreciate the ones you win.

Your language plays an essential role in your ability to reinforce your mindset to stay the course. When you encounter adversity, do you see it as a setback? A setback implies moving backward. Do you see it as a problem? A problem implies trouble or difficulty. What would happen if you saw adversity as a challenge? A challenge suggests that special effort is required to achieve a goal. Your word choice impacts the way your mind perceives the task before you. Perception becomes reality. One person can see an event as a tragedy, and another person's perception is that it is an inconvenience. Which person is more likely to persevere?

If you haven't achieved your goal, you have more to learn. You have skills to be further developed. You have beliefs that must shift. There is more action to take. You are always exactly where you are supposed to be.

Perseverance isn't something that has an end date. You don't accomplish a goal, and then life is smooth sailing from there. The secret is to balance your emotional state through the ups and downs. No matter what comes your way, you keep moving forward. You have faith and trust in your ability to figure out a way to get there. You build a boat, or you swim to get off the island. When you understand the significance of what's on the other side of perseverance, you will stop at nothing to reach your reward.

More Heart Than Talent

Many people in the world are talented. It is a misconception that it requires talent to be successful. Talent is important when it comes to performing, but the path to success in entrepreneurship has little to do with talent. It has more to do with having grit and having heart. To break through, you have to get out of your talent. You have to stop hiding behind it. You have to take risks, be vulnerable, and let go of perfection.

When you lead from your heart, you won't let fear stop you. You won't hesitate or procrastinate. Procrastination comes from fear of not being perfect. It perpetuates low self-esteem because you believe you are not good enough to be successful. You live in unwarranted perfection. Procrastination leads to disappointment because it keeps you avoiding your dreams.

Living in your heart begins with living in the moment. You begin to make moves before you are ready. You let go of limiting beliefs. You stand tall in the face of adversity. You take on life's challenges because you are committed to the outcome. Having heart takes courage. Without courage, you will tiptoe through life quietly to arrive at your grave safely living the pain of regret.

Heart is what separates the average from the exceptional. Heart is the ability to push through what you resist. It is your ability to get out of your comfort zone and leave your miserable zone. When you come from your heart, you are not in your mind processing. When you are in your heart, you are out of your ego. When you come from ego, you aren't willing to be vulnerable. To break through, you have to believe in your human potential. You have to believe you deserve to be successful.

I host a one-day event called More Heart Than Talent an average of forty times year. I host this event all over the United States. The people that are attracted to this event are seeking a breakthrough. The content I deliver is the very content you are reading in this book. I teach how to break down the cause and effect of why you do what you do. I assist people to understand how the events in their life have shaped their feelings and behaviors. I show them how to let go and lead from their heart.

I also host a workshop four times a year called

Breakthroughs to Success. This event is only for my personal coaching clients. This weekend is designed for people with a heartfelt desire to take their lives and businesses to the next level. I have an exercise I do with my students that I adapted from my alcohol rehab experience. I call it "the circle." In the middle of the circle is a special chair called "the love seat." Together we address past events, self-talk, and physical and emotional addictions. We address the cause and effect of why you do you do in life and business. This exercise breaks down barriers and creates bonds between the attendees that last a lifetime.

In June 2005, a client of mine came to Breakthroughs to Success. I asked him to bring his guitar to sing and play for the event. This client had endured severe abuse as a child but found music as an outlet. He started by playing a song he had written, and he captivated the crowd. After he finished, I embraced him and told him, "That was freakin' awesome." My client received so much unconditional love from the strangers in the room that he became overwhelmed. The following morning, he drove three hours home instead of finishing the last day of the event. After being home for a few hours, something told him to come back. When he returned, he walked into the room, and the whole group surrounded him. They hugged him and once again showed him unconditional love. This was the beginning of his breakthrough. He began to address the events from his past, his addictions, and lack of self-love. I have had the honor of hiring him to come back to my events to provide music for the group. I've watched him continue to break through in his life and music. He was so inspired by the breakthrough process that he wrote a song called "More Heart Than Talent." He has given me permission to print the lyrics in this book.

More Heart Than Talent
I walk into the room my head is to the floor,
I wonder what it is that I've been looking for?
When I look around at the faces in the circle,
Jeff says out loud, "Leave your ego at the door."
I feel a lot of fear when I have to take my mask off.
As the layers they unfold, I feel naked and alone.
But then I hear the voices gathered round the circle.
They say you're not alone, welcome to your home.

I have more heart than talent, it's way down deep in my soul.
I have more heart than talent; I'm getting closer to my goals.
I have more heart than talent; I look into my heart, I look into my heart; I look into my heart, and make a brand new start.

It took a lot of courage; it took a lot of friends.
I took a lot of turns; I took a lot of bends.
No, I'm not a victim, and no, I'm not ashamed.

I'm living in my power; I'm living in my game.
I'm living loving life, a feeling that's within.
A millionaire mindset, you know I'm gonna win.
The Universe is mine, the power never ends.
Pixie dust and Jen are my forever friends.

I have more heart than talent, it's way down deep
in my soul.
I have more heart than talent; I'm getting closer
to my goals.
I have more heart than talent; I look into my
heart, I look into my heart; I look into my heart,
and make a brand new start.[15]

Being outside of your talent is the hands-free zone.
It is a state of flow. It is a relaxed state of consciousness.
It means you love who you are. You love who you
are becoming and what you are doing. You become
comfortable with who you are becoming. When you
make this shift, you tap into your heart consciousness—
talent is not required.

Moving into Flow

The moment you recognize you are stuck, you are
having a breakthrough. What was once unconscious
now becomes conscious. You have the opportunity to
move out of stuckness and into forward motion. You
take one step and then take another until you begin to
glide forward. This is how you begin to move into flow.

Taking the first steps are not always easy. It means

you leave your comfort zone. You shed your old skin. You leave the nest. You make the choice to become the new you. The more your consciousness expands, the more your forward motion will follow as you take action steps. Stuart Wilde details this idea in his book *The Little Money Bible: The Ten Laws of Abundance.*

> The action of flow is one of being alive and aware, ready to step forward fearlessly. You have to move toward your target. So do something each and every day that improves your situation and takes you closer to your dream. Sometimes that action may just be a simple thing that grants you more stability, or more order—like perhaps you take a day out to tidy up your paperwork. Order of itself is a positive thing, is it not?
>
> Rarely do opportunities find you; usually you have to be moving toward them. So heighten your ability to stay in the flow by heading out, talking to people, making contacts, stepping out from where it's safe and cozy, pushing against your comfort zones, reaching out. That's how the faucet of flow is turned on—by generating energy each day so the Universe-at-Large can engage its magnificent laws and deliver to you even more energy.[16]

Flow comes from movement, not from stagnancy. If you are stagnant in an area of your life, it is time to get moving. The challenge many people have is that when they start moving, it feels uncomfortable. Life becomes unpredictable. They are unable to control the outcome. It can be so uncomfortable that they retreat back to the known—the state of stuckness that is familiar. To move into flow, you must be willing to take off the hundred pound backpack that contains your limiting beliefs, past events, and emotional states that no longer serve you. As you let go of this weight, you will move from baby steps to walking, then to running, and some of you may learn how to fly. Increased consciousness coupled with action is what moves you into flow.

Breakthroughs as a Way of Life

Breaking through is not a one-time event. There is always another layer to peel back on the onion. When you make breakthroughs a way of life, the compounded effect will take place. Each breakthrough builds upon the last. You start to see and understand people, situations, and most importantly yourself more quickly. Each breakthrough raises your level of consciousness.

As these changes start to occur, you break through your emotional barriers. It becomes a way of life. Breaking through is not physical. Breaking through is emotional. When you are breaking through, you have aha moments frequently. Your reality changes. Vishen Lakhaini, founder of Mindvalley, discusses this concept in his book, *The Code of the Extraordinary Mind*.

All growth comes from changing your models of reality to upgrading a system for living. Changing a model of reality is a form of growth that often comes from epiphany or insight. It's a sudden awakening or revelation that shifts a belief. Once you adopt a new model of reality that is superior to an older model, you can't go back.[17]

As you make shifts in consciousness, inspiration will surface. Facing challenges becomes easier. You do what's required to find a solution. In this state of consciousness, you will attract other like-minded, inspired success seekers.

Every day you receive 1,444 minutes. How do you want to spend them? Addicted to the past or committed to your recovery? Do you want to spend them blaming others for your circumstances or taking responsibility for your feelings? Do you want to live a life of regret or a life of inspired action?

To break through, you must surrender and let go on a daily basis. I have thirty-plus years of sobriety from drugs and alcohol. I find forgiveness for others and myself each day. I'm checked into life. I am no longer the mind-body connection to the events and transgressions that led to my addictions.

Breaking through is a commitment to yourself to live your best life. It starts with a decision—one minute, one hour, one day at a time.

Ask Yourself

1. What price am I willing to pay to achieve my goals?

2. What impact will it have on my life if I don't achieve my goals? What impact will it have on my life if I do achieve my goals?
3. What actions can I take daily to live an inspired life?

FOR COMPANION RESOURCES, GO TO
https://goldenmastermind.com/breakthrough-factor
Digital Coaching Mini-Course

NOTES

1. David Hawkins, *Power vs. Force: The Hidden Determinants of Human Behavior* (Carlsbad, Calif.: Hay House, 2014), 80.

2. Neel Burton, MD, "Self-Deception Series: Repression and Denial," *Psychology Today*, March 5, 2012; https://www.psychologytoday.com/us/blog/hide-and-seek/201203/self-deception-series-repression-and-denial.

3. Dr. Joe Dispenza, *Breaking The Habit of Being Yourself: How to Lose Your Mind and Create a New One* (Carlsbad, Calif.: Hay House, 2013), p. 151.

4. Hawkins, *Power vs Force*, p. 80.

5. Hawkins, *Power vs. Force*, pp. 79-80.

6. David R. Hawkins, *Transcending the Levels of Consciousness: The Stairway to Enlightenment* (Carlsbad, Calif.: Hay House, 2006), p. 30.

7. Nancy Colier, "Can We Get Addicted to Disappointment?" *Psychology Today*, August 15, 2016; https://www.psychologytoday.com/us/blog/inviting-monkey-tea/201608/can-we-get-addicted-disappointment.

8. David R. Hawkins, MD, PhD, *Letting Go: The Pathway to Surrender* (Carlsbad, Calif.: Hay House, 2014), pp. 20–21.

9. Bruce H. Lipton, PhD, Unleashing the Power of the Consciousness, Matter & Miracles (Carlsbad, Calif.: Hay House, 2005), p. 98.

10. Catherine Ponder, *The Dynamic Laws of Prosperity* (Upper Saddle River, New Jersey: Prentice Hall, 1962), pp. 19–20.

11. Simon Sinek, *Start with Why: How Great Leaders Inspire Everyone to Take Action* (New York: Penguin, 2009), pp.65–66.

12. Colin Tipping, *Radical Forgiveness* (Boulder, Colo.: Sounds True, Inc., 2009), p. 47.

13. Dispenza, *Breaking the Habit of Being Yourself,* p. 59.

14. Ponder, *The Dynamic Laws of Prosperity*, pp.40–41.

15. Permission given by Robert Grijalva to include lyrics; https://store.cdbaby.com/cd/robertanthony2.

16. Stuart Wilde, *The Little Money Bible: The Ten Laws of Abundance* (Carlsbad, Calif.: Hay House, 1998), p. 17.

17. Vishen Lakhaini, *The Code of the Extraordinary Mind* (New York: Rodale, 2016) p. 61.

 JEFFERY COMBS is an internationally recognized trainer, speaker, and best-selling author in the areas of sales, marketing, branding, and addiction. Jeff specializes in prospecting, leadership, scripts, spirituality, personal breakthroughs, mindset training, consciousness, and all levels of effective marketing. His many audio training programs benefit entrepreneurs and direct sales people at all levels of conscious development.

Jeff has consulted with over 9,000 clients as a personal coach and mentor and has devoted over 55,000 hours to his personal coaching practice. He is highly sought after by entrepreneurs, direct sales people, network marketers, and people from all walks of life. The president of Golden Mastermind Seminars Inc., Jeff is committed to assisting people change the way they feel in order to achieve their goals and dreams.

Jeff is available to you and your company for coaching and speaking, and he has developed a special package of training materials and professional guidance that will assist you and your team to create maximum results now. For further information, please call 800-595-6632 or visit his website at www. goldenmastermind.com.

YOU DESERVE TO HAVE IT ALL!

Personal Coaching
Producers Package
with Jeffery Combs

Jeffery Combs is the President and CEO of Golden Mastermind Seminars Inc. He is an internationally recognized trainer, speaker, and best-selling author specializing in sales, marketing, branding, and addiction. He has personally coached thousands of entrepreneurs and industry leaders, and he is committed to assisting people to change the way they feel in order to achieve their goals and dreams. Jeffery specializes in a 2-1/2 day workshop called Breakthroughs To Success. This is an absolute must for anyone desiring to go to the next level.

The Producers Package Includes:

- 5 Hours Personal Coaching with Jeffery Combs
- 1 Breakthroughs To Success Weekend Event Ticket
- 1 Digital Mastermind Library

800-595-6632
www.GoldenMastermind.com

GOLDEN MASTERMIND SEMINARS, INC.
THE DIGITAL MASTERMIND LIBRARY

With over 100 hours of content from Jeffery Combs and his guest speakers, this is your ULTIMATE empowering training library! Owning the complete Mastermind Library is a must for anyone serious about building an enterprise!

- Receive Full Access to the **NEW** Digital Library at 65% OFF
- 22 training audios, 6 e-books, and The Millionaire Tip Lab
- All content is now MOBILE FRIENDLY!
- Receive New, Never Before Seen Training from Jeff's Archives!

Total Retail Value Exceeds $2,000.00!
Special *Anger Factor* Discounted Offer Only $697.00

www.GoldenMastermind.com/platinum-level-access

DIGITAL COACHING COURSE

The Jeffery Combs Digital Coaching Program is as eye-opening as it is rewarding. Each module is taught by Jeffery Combs, sought after success coach and industry expert, and is facilitated through short videos and assignments. There are 8 modules and the course is designed for you to complete one module per week.

Those that fully engage and complete the program will emerge with the habits and mindset to be successful... And also have the tools and resilience to move freely through the challenges of business and life.

TOTAL RETAIL VALUE EXCEEDS $2000!
SPECIAL MORE HEART THAN TALENT DISCOUNTED OFFER ONLY $997

JEFFERYCOMBSDIGITALCOACHING.COM

Made in the USA
San Bernardino, CA
15 January 2019